# How to Add an EXTRA Bathroom

## A COMPLETE GUIDE TO HOME PLUMBING

**Donald R. Brann**

Library of Congress Card No. 68-18108

SIXTH PRINTING — 1976
REVISED EDITION

Published by
**DIRECTIONS SIMPLIFIED, INC.**

Division of
**EASI-BILD PATTERN CO., INC.
Briarcliff Manor, NY 10510**

FIRST PRINTING
© 1968

REVISED EDITIONS
1971,1972,1973,1974,
1976


ISBN 0-87733-682-2

NOTE
Due to the variance in quality and availability of many materials and products, always follow directions a manufacturer and/or retailer offers. Unless products are used exactly as the manufacturer specifies, its warranty can be voided. While the author mentions certain products by trade name, no endorsement or end use guarantee is implied. In every case the author suggests end uses as specified by the manufacturer prior to publication.

Since manufacturers frequently change ingredients or formula and/or introduce new and improved products, or fail to distribute in certain areas, trade names are mentioned to help the reader zero in on products of comparable quality and end use. The Publisher.

# Adding an Extra Bathroom Isn't Splurging... It's Living!

So states one of the country's largest banks in promoting home improvement loans. Like most financial institutions interested in lending money, this bank believes a bathroom installation is not only a sound investment, an asset that pays immediate dividends in comfort and convenience, but also one that invariably pays a handsome Capital Gains when the house is sold.

If your family needs an extra bathroom, don't fight it. Don't allow bathroom congestion to be a daily irritant. Installing an extra toilet, lavatory, bathtub or shower isn't a "big deal," when you know how it's done. Nor need it be considered an expense. The fixtures and materials required represent a capital investment. Knowing how the job is done permits pricing everything — fixtures, fittings, etc., prior to purchase. It also permits buying as much skilled help as you need. Buying a bathroom installation, without knowing cost of components, is like buying a pig in a poke.

Installing an extra bathroom will, at first, seem like a frightening experience. This is natural because most everything we do for the first time, whether it's learning to ride a bike, drive a car or fly a plane, creates fear, and this is as it should be. Fear stimulates the senses. It also separates the men from the boys. Those who continually attempt jobs they have never previously tried, continue to grow. These are God's chosen children, people considered lucky. Those who frighten easily, who chicken out, begin to die long before they have learned to live.

This book helps you build a bigger and better individual. It also helps you install a complete bathroom for "peanuts," when compared to the inflated estimates you'll get from fast buck home improvers.

Knowing how any problem can be solved, then doing something about it, is the key to good health, happiness and peace of mind. If any problem frightens you, take action. Doing is for the living. Those who try living more, fear less.

# TABLE OF CONTENTS

# INTRODUCTION

Since every family has its own special needs and ideas, and every house presents a different configuration of pipe, fittings, and placement of fixtures, this book doesn't suggest installing A BATHROOM IN A LOCATION. It does explain every facet of the work that needs to be done. You must select location, plan fixture placement, make connections to existing lines. For these basic reasons, you must read this book completely, not once, but two, three, even four times. Place a check mark alongside each paragraph, underline sentences, that relate to what you want to do. Consult the glossary on page 156 to become familiar with fittings and accessories. And remember, the greatest accomplishment and the longest trip, requires taking the first step.

Because new products now simplify plumbing, the installation of a bathroom is a project every family can successfully accomplish if they read and follow directions. While a plumber's furnace, molten lead, and a calking iron are needed to install cast iron hub and spigot pipe, today, no-hub cast iron can be installed by anyone who has a ⅝″ end wrench.

The most important part of this job is to select and install fittings recommended, in position illustrated. Use pipe sizes, install vent and drainage lines according to local codes.

This book will help you select a location, frame walls, position fixtures, use proper fittings, provide answers to problems you never previously faced.

Many handy homeowners will obtain all the information they need by referring to about six illustrations. Others, seeking complete freedom from plumbing repair bills, will study each illustration when mentioned, and will learn the many different ways they can economically install an extra bathroom, as well as solve plumbing problems.

# HOW TO CONCEIVE AN EXTRA BATHROOM
# WITH MINIMAL PLUMBING PAINS

Plumbing and numbered painting have much in common. Where numbered colors are applied to areas specified, in sequence directions suggest, this book illustrates fittings and explains procedure required to simplify installation. Learning how this job is done permits readers to act as a plumber's helper. They do only as much work as he or she feels capable of doing. Since only part of a bathroom installation concerns actual plumbing, there are many parts of the job a reader can do. After learning How, doing what you can, offers unlimited opportunities for making sizable savings.

The reader must discover where pipes are concealed in a wall, decide where fixtures are to be placed and what fittings are needed.

Making an installation against an existing wall, or within a new wall is usually the easiest. In every case, plasterboard or flooring that's removed must be replaced and all exposed pipes enclosed either in a dummy wall or enclosure, or cabinet, bookcase, etc.

Placing fixtures where you want them, rather than close to an existing soil and vent stack, increases cost for pipe and extra fittings, but this is peanuts compared to the added value of the completed bathroom.

While this book was conceived as a guide for homeowners who want to do all the work, the easy-to-understand technical data helps homeowners effect sizeable savings if they contract part or all of the work.

Installing an extra bathroom is a big time business, currently infested with high pressure con men. Play safe, don't discuss any home improvement job except with an established retailer! Don't consider TV, radio, and other "special offers." *

Regard this project as an interesting experience in home ownership, or as a new business opportunity. Anyone who learns how this job is done, and does it, can earn a good living doing it for others. Since most solvent homeowners can get their mortgage refinanced to include the cost of a new bathroom, it offers unlimited potential.

---

* If in doubt, call the Better Business Bureau.

Before applying for a home improvement loan, before buying fixtures, before asking a plumber or carpenter for an estimate, learn the "word game." Become familiar with the various fittings, pipe sizes, vent and waste lines. Only when you become familiar with procedure can you talk intelligently to a "pro." If he knows you know what needs to be done, he will, if he wants the work, quote an estimate close to what you will find acceptable. Let him tell you why he likes, or dislikes, the location you have selected for an extra bathroom, whether he concurs with the plan you have laid out for a waste or vent line.

## WHAT PRICE JOHN?

As every banker will tell you, expanding a house to add more living space is a sound investment. Adding a comfortable size bathroom is a better investment than an economy size.

A bathroom can cost almost anything you want to pay. The cost is dependent on these factors: quality of fixtures, distance from sewer line, pipe and fittings required; and most important, how well you read, and how much work you are willing to do. Since this book tells HOW to do it, overall costs depend on how much you do, how much you are willing to pay to have it done. To zero in on the exact work your installation requires, place a check mark alongside every paragraph, and/or illustration, that pertains to your job.

To find out what an extra bathroom really costs, price quality fixtures, materials, and labor separately. Then call in one, two, or three reputable home improvers, and get ready for a shock. Ask them to estimate on a complete job:
1. Plumbing
2. Carpentry
3. Wiring
4. Installation of fixtures and equipment you select
5. Ceramic tile on floor and walls
6. Wallboard inside and out, also on ceiling if required
7. Painting

Be sure to specify exact area you want tiled. Specify quality of tile for walls and floor.

## THE CHOICE IS YOURS, THE SAVINGS TERRIFIC

Up to a short time ago, there was only one way to install an extra bathroom. Today there are three. You can make an installation like it has always been done, i.e. select a location adjacent to a wall containing the soil stack, Illus. 1.

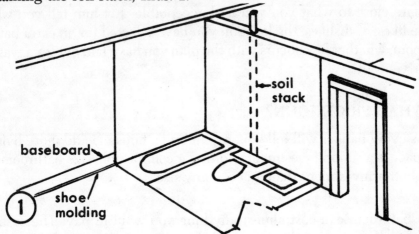

First decide whether you want to connect to present soil and vent stack, or whether you want to run a new one. Next decide whether you want to run the new one on the outside of an existing wall or between the studs; or between studs of new wall frame needed to enclose bathroom. In either case, remove shoe molding and baseboard and finished flooring within area selected. Removing finished flooring permits installing waterproof plywood and ceramic tile on top of existing sub-flooring, and still allow tile floor to finish flush with adjoining floor.

To connect to an existing soil line, remove sub-flooring and plaster or plasterboard on walls containing plumbing. Since you will also have to install cats and backerboards for lavatory, tub controls, etc., we recommend removing wallboard from entire wall. Doing this simplifies roughing-in plumbing, wiring, framing required for fan or heater, etc., Illus. 2, 3.

If you plan on placing fixtures on two walls, remove sub-flooring where it is necessary to rough-in plumbing. If fixtures are placed on one wall, it's sometimes possible to only remove sub-flooring between two joists.

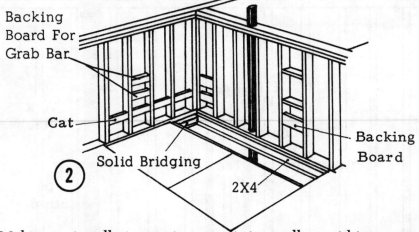

Backing Board For Grab Bar

Cat

Solid Bridging

Backing Board

2X4

(2)

Making an installation against an existing wall, or within a new wall is usually the easiest. In every case, plasterboard or flooring that's removed must be replaced and all exposed pipes enclosed either in a dummy wall or enclosure, or cabinet, bookcase, etc.

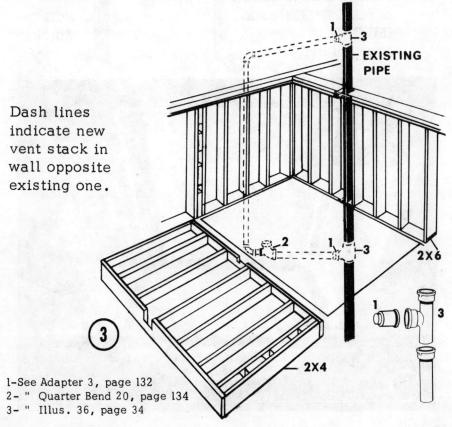

Dash lines indicate new vent stack in wall opposite existing one.

EXISTING PIPE

2X6

2X4

(3)

1-See Adapter 3, page 132
2- "  Quarter Bend 20, page 134
3- "  Illus. 36, page 34

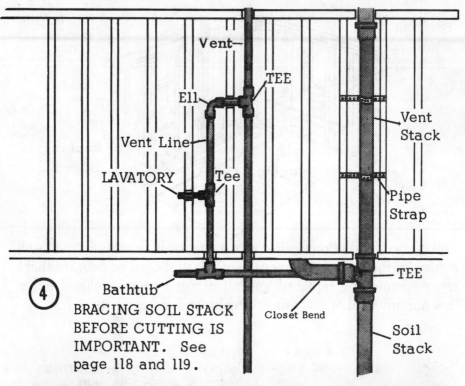

Vent

TEE

Ell

Vent Line

LAVATORY

Tee

Vent
Stack

Pipe
Strap

(4) Bathtub

TEE

Closet Bend

BRACING SOIL STACK
BEFORE CUTTING IS
IMPORTANT. See
page 118 and 119.

Soil
Stack

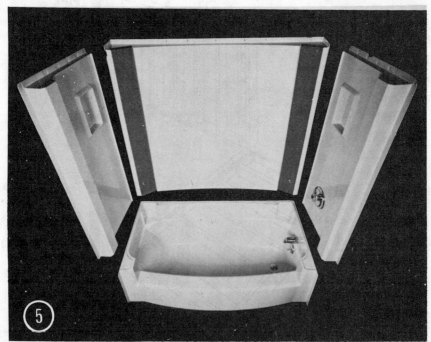

(5)

The second choice, one that cuts on the job installation time to a minimum, is the pre-fabricated fiber glass bathtub, that comes KD (knocked down), Illus. 5, in four sections that are clipped together, Illus. 6.° We call this unit the Instant Bathtub since everything that can be done is done at the factory. The reinforced fiber glass unit contains tub, three walls and shower. Available with tub drain on left or right end, the unit can be installed by anyone within the framing specified, Illus. 7. Installation of this unit is described on page 100.

*Due to continual changes in design, always follow manufacturers directions when installing equipment.

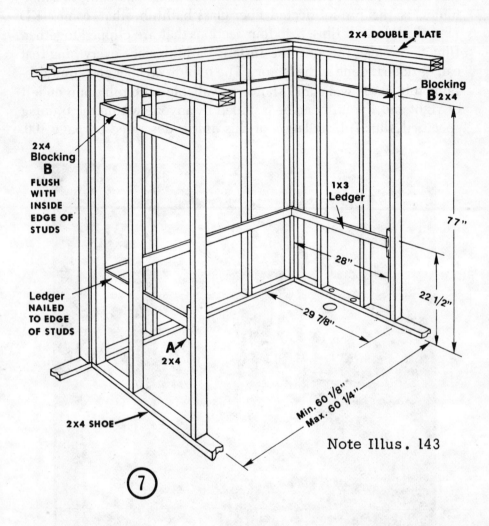

2x4 DOUBLE PLATE

Blocking
B 2x4

2x4
Blocking
B
FLUSH
WITH
INSIDE
EDGE OF
STUDS

1X3
Ledger

77"

Ledger
NAILED
TO EDGE
OF STUDS

28"

22 1/2"

29 7/8"

A
2x4

Min. 60 1/8"
Max. 60 1/4"

2x4 SHOE

Note Illus. 143

⑦

The third choice, the EB Pre-Engineered Plumbing Wall, Illus. 8, eliminates a good two thirds of the work on the job. This approach provides the core required to service any size bathroom you want to install. The unit comes directly from factory completely assembled in a 2x6 wall frame. You can recess this unit, frame and all, into an existing wall, Illus. 9; against an existing wall, Illus. 12; or use it as a room divider, Illus. 10, with a bathroom on one or both sides, a bedroom or lavatory on the other; or a dressing room, or kitchen, Illus. 11.

14

Since the plumbing wall is shipped complete with a wall hung toilet, a bathtub and lavatory that drains into wall inlets, installation requires drilling only four holes; one for 3″ waste line, one for 3″ vent line, and two ½″ water lines. While 3″ copper tubing and a roof flange are supplied for venting this unit, no below floor tubing or fittings are supplied. These must be purchased locally.

Directions for ordering and installing this unit is described on pages 90 and 119.

The fiber glass bathtub and the EB Plumbing Wall, Illus. 6, 8, makes Instant Heroes out of homeowners who install it themselves.

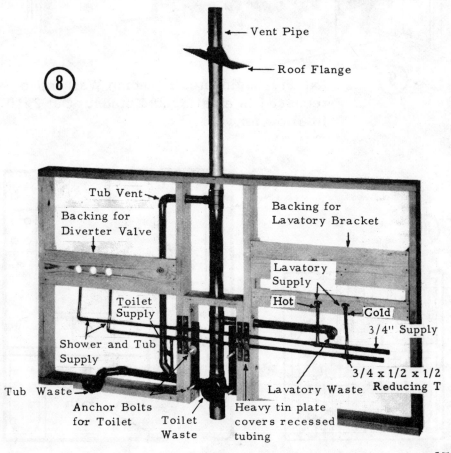

Vent Pipe

Roof Flange

⑧

Tub Vent

Backing for Diverter Valve

Backing for Lavatory Bracket

Lavatory Supply

Hot

Cold

3/4″ Supply

Toilet Supply

Shower and Tub Supply

3/4 x 1/2 x 1/2 Reducing T

Tub Waste

Anchor Bolts for Toilet

Toilet Waste

Lavatory Waste

Heavy tin plate covers recessed tubing

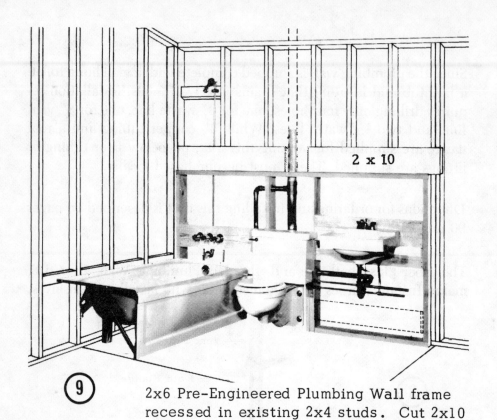

⑨ 2x6 Pre-Engineered Plumbing Wall frame
recessed in existing 2x4 studs. Cut 2x10
to allow for vent.

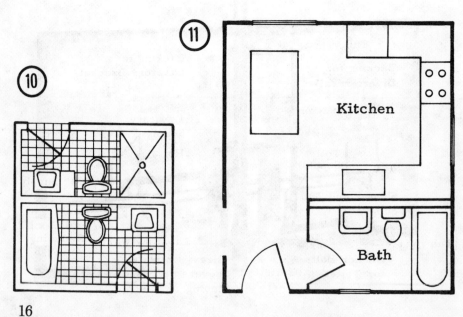

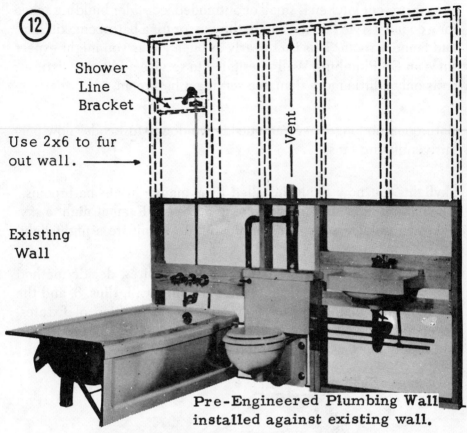

(12)

Shower
Line
Bracket

Use 2x6 to fur
out wall. ———→

Vent

Existing
Wall

**Pre-Engineered Plumbing Wall**
**installed against existing wall.**

## WHERE – WHEN – HOW

Since finding space for an extra bathroom and its cost are two of
your first problems, consider these economic facts of present day
life. The population explosion, plus the continually rising cost of
labor, materials, etc., makes every home improvement a sound, long
term investment. Most homeowners who keep up mortgage pay-
ments can get it refinanced to pay for any major improvement.

Building an addition is, in most cases, a far better investment than
buying a larger house. It provides one of the easiest ways to add one
or two bedrooms, plus a bathroom. This approach usually permits
making a connection to the sewer without disturbing any walls or
floors. It also permits locating the new bathroom anywhere that's
convenient, providing the new sewer line slopes at least ¼" to each
foot of run.

If your present kitchen is small or outmoded, consider building space for a country style kitchen and bathroom; or for a bathroom, kitchen[1] and laundry room. This isn't nearly as big a job as you might expect since an EB Plumbing Wall[2], designed to service additional fixtures, costs only a little more than one serving a bathroom.

Bathrooms no longer need an outside window. Most codes now permit ventilating fans.

Skylights[3] are now being installed over many "inside bathrooms." The natural light simplifies applying make-up. Even at night a skylight can provide sufficient illumination to eliminate a night light.

After selecting location for bathroom and fixtures, decide method of roughing-in. The pre-engineered plumbing wall, Illus. 8, and the pre-fabricated bathtub, Illus. 6, predetermine position of fixtures. When installing either one, make a connection to vent and soil stack, and supply lines, wherever it's most convenient.

(13)

[1]See Easi-Bild Book L08-608, How to Modernize a Kitchen.
[2]See page 92.
[3]Book L65-665, How to Modernize an Attic, tells HOW to install a skylight.

Either unit can be placed in, or against, an existing wall; against or in one of the new wall frames needed to enclose bathroom. A vent line could be installed between joists in attic, the soil line between floor joists, then connected to existing soil stack.

It's important to study every illustration since each explains much about basic plumbing — where to use 4″ cast iron or 3″ copper; the size of vent and drainage lines. Equally important, if you know what the plumber or plumbing supply retailer is talking about, and he knows you know, a meeting of the minds takes place, and both parties benefit without time consuming, costly conversation.

If you decide to expand your house to obtain space for a bathroom, follow step-by-step directions outlined in Easi-Bild Add-A-Room Book L09-609. This book tells how to build a 12x16, 16x24, or any smaller or larger size room with either a gable, Illus. 13, or shed type roof, Illus. 14. If you plan on installing a bathroom in an attic or basement, Easi-Bild Books L03-603, How to Build a Dormer; L65-665, How to Modernize an Attic; and L15-615, How to Modernize a Basement; explain every step. Each takes the fear, mystery, and more than half the cost out of these important home improvements.

If your house is built on a concrete slab, or over an inaccessible crawl space, you can obtain needed pitch for waste line by following this procedure. Install 2x6 or 2x8 joists over existing floor. Run joists parallel to 3″ or 4″ waste line, Illus. 15. Nail ¾″ exterior grade plywood to joists. This provides a good base for ceramic tile. Another way is to use the EB pre-engineered plumbing wall, Illus. 8.

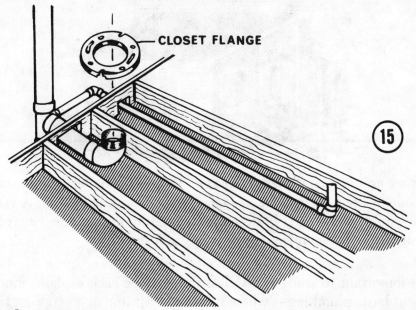

CLOSET FLANGE

(15)

Study your present bathroom so you can decide what you want in a new one. Use the fixture template and grid, pages 121, 159, to simplify drawing up a plan. Allow a minimum of 15″ from a side wall to center of a toilet.

Installing an extra bathroom with stock fixtures follows this basic procedure:
1. Select location
2. Lay out position of fixtures — toilet, lavatory, bathtub.
3. Remove flooring, plaster or plasterboard on walls where required.
4. Frame walls needed to enclose room. Provide backing for bathtub, grab bars, shower curtain sockets, lavatory; framing for ventilating fan, heater, etc.
5. Rough-in closet bend, soil line to sewer connection, waste, vent and supply lines; heating; duct to outside wall (if required) for ventilating fan.

6. Rough-in electrical lines for lighting, wall outlets, fan, heater, etc.

7. Nail cats, backerboards where required, lay plyscord sub-flooring.

8. Set bathtub, connect tub to trap, drainage, vent and supply lines.

9. Apply vinyl faced gypsum board to walls around bathtub, also on walls to be tiled.

10. Apply regular gypsum board to walls that are to be painted or wallpapered, and to ceiling, or install luminous ceiling[1]

11. Apply prefinished plywood[2], or gypsum board to exterior walls of bathroom.

12. Apply ceramic wall tile[3], around tub, then other walls.

13. Lay mosaic tile on floor.

14. Install medicine chest, light fixtures, soap trays, towel and grab bars, fan, heater, etc., following manufacturer's directions.

15. Install toilet, lavatory.

16. Hang door, apply trim, paint, wallpaper, etc.

[1]See Book L94-694, Electrical Repairs Simplified
[2]See Book L05-605, How to Apply Paneling
[3]See Book L06-606, How to Lay Ceramic Tile

Don't start this job until you have planned the entire installation. If you find yourself stumped by any step, ask your plumbing supply dealer to explain. Since the illustrations in this book cover most important areas, refer to those pertinent to your problem.

Don't continue working after you get tired. A clear head is required to successfully do something you have never done before. Don't rush. Take plenty of time. If in doubt, stop, ask.

Because copper, no-hub cast iron, PVC or ABS[1] plastic is easy to install, use 3" for sewer line, 1½" or 2" for drainage and vents.

[1]PVC—Poly Vinyl Chloride and ABS—Acrylonitrile-butadiene-styrene are two of today's most important developments. Both greatly simplify plumbing. See page 89 for easy-to-install directions.

Those who tried soldering during manual training classes and were unsuccessful, have a pleasant surprise coming. Today, joining copper sweat fittings and plastic tubing is real easy.

If you are still hesitant, buy a length of ½" copper tubing, a few fittings and practice. Follow detailed directions outlined on page 83. After joining, make a water test. If unsuccessful, apply heat and take each connection apart. Clean up pipe and fittings and try again.

If sweating copper is not for you, use PVC — polyvinyl chloride plastic pipe, Illus. 61. This is even easier to install than copper. Directions on page 89 explain every step. Fittings that correspond to those available in cast iron and/or copper are available. PVC pipe can be joined to cast iron or copper. Most updated codes permit PVC to be used in the same size as copper.

The answers to many problems, particularly the selection of proper fittings, can be found by studying your present plumbing.

Before buying pipe, fittings and fixtures, make certain you understand how the job is done, and have decided you will make the installation. If you hire a plumber to help, make certain he is willing to use your materials.

If you hire a plumber, have him write down what he agrees to do. If he agrees to "rough-in and set fixtures," this means making a test, after he completes roughing-in, to make certain there are no leaks. Roughing-in refers to all lines, waste, vent and water. It also requires his coming back when the tiling is completed, to set and connect fixtures. Since you may be delayed in completing the tiling, be sure he's willing to take part payment when roughing-in is completed, balance when fixtures are set and operable.

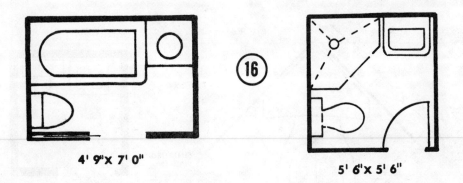

4' 9"x 7' 0"

5' 6"x 5' 6"

A WORD ABOUT WORDS. To clarify directions, we call a water closet a toilet, a wash basin a lavatory. To further simplify visualizing each step, every fitting and fixture is illustrated and designated by trade name. Ask for these by name. This approach stimulates cooperation from busy plumbing supply sales clerks. Note reference guides on pages 132,155.

Space saving fixtures, a corner bathtub, corner lavatory and corner toilet, Illus. 16, 17, require minimum space. A 4'0" closet can be converted into a powder room, Illus 18.

A minimum size bathroom can be made operable in less than 35 square feet, Illus. 16.

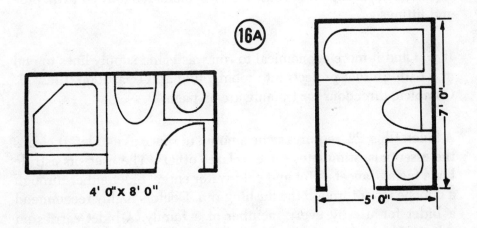

4' 0"x 8' 0"

7' 0"

5' 0"

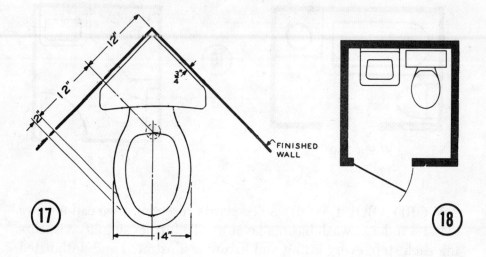

FINISHED WALL

(17) (18)

A multiple use bathroom, Illus. 19, requiring approximately 90 square feet, is a sound investment. Separate shower stall, corner bathtub, toilet privacy partition, and two lavatories provide a lot of convenience.

Illus. 20 shows a double bathroom designed for a large family. Doors can be repositioned to provide access to a bedroom or hall.

Placement of fixtures along one wall, as indicated in Illus. 16A, 18, provides an economical way to "rough-in" plumbing. The cost of installing fixtures shown in Illus. 19, 20, is increased only by extra pipe and fittings.

If you find it more economical to run waste and supply lines to end of a bathtub that projects into room, build a 2x4 partition, Illus. 21. Complete directions for framing are on page 40.

A bidet, Illus. 22, requires same amount of space as a toilet. It cleans the essentials, stimulates some, relaxes others. The user sits astride bowl facing faucets. Hot and cold water enters bidet either through a douche jet or through the flushing rim. Doctors highly recommend a bidet for use by every member of a family. A bidet carries no solids. Most codes permit using an 1½" P-Trap.

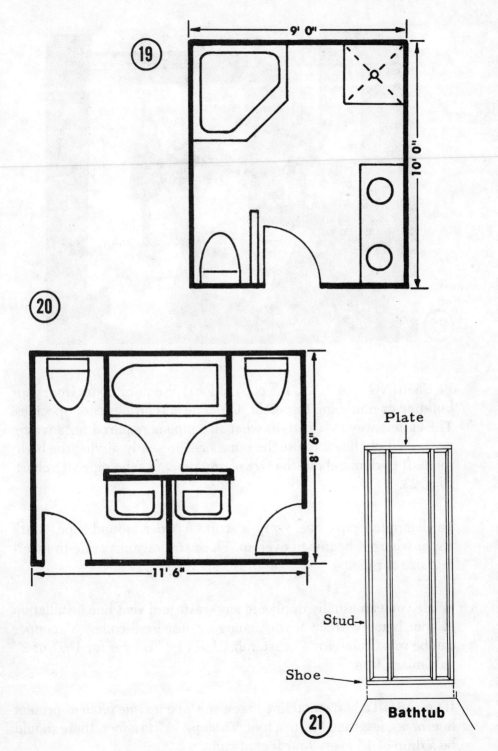

⑲

9' 0"

10' 0"

⑳

8' 6"

11' 6"

㉑

Plate

Stud

Shoe

**Bathtub**

PLUMBING CODES. Get a copy of local plumbing codes from your building or plumbing inspector. Use pipe and fittings code specifies. The easiest way to ascertain what size pipe is required for a waste, vent or supply line is to use the same size, presently serving the bathroom. If in doubt about the size of any pipe, use the pipe size chart, Illus. 23.

To determine pipe size, wrap a strip of paper around pipe. Mark paper where it begins to overlap. Place strip against scale to ascertain size of pipe.

While you can usually duplicate any waste and vent line installation in your home without fear of going against local codes, 3″ copper can be substituted for 4″ cast iron; 1½″ or 2″ copper for 1½″ or 2″ galvanized iron.

If you install a horizontal line to sewer, slope it same pitch as present line, or not less than ¼″ to a foot. To slope ¼″ to a foot, there should be a drop of 1″ every four feet of run.

26

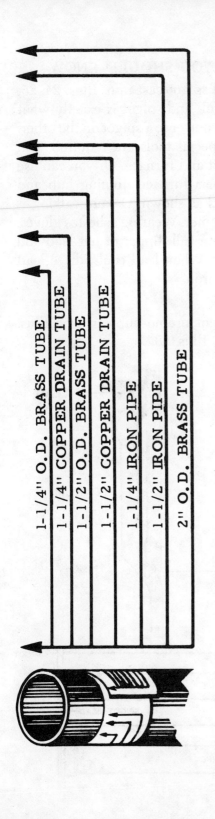

1-1/4" O.D. BRASS TUBE

1-1/4" COPPER DRAIN TUBE

1-1/2" O.D. BRASS TUBE

1-1/2" COPPER DRAIN TUBE

1-1/4" IRON PIPE

1-1/2" IRON PIPE

2" O.D. BRASS TUBE

HANDY PIPE SIZING SCALE. To determine size, wrap a strip of paper around pipe. Mark overlap then check size below for copper tube.

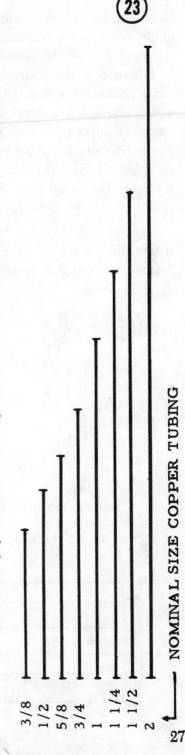

3/8
1/2
5/8
3/4
1
1 1/4
1 1/2
2

NOMINAL SIZE COPPER TUBING

# TOOLS, FITTINGS, AND FACTS YOU SHOULD KNOW

Until you learn how, joining hub and spigot cast iron, Illus. 24, 25, might seem like a frightening job. Hub and spigot is exactly what the name implies. It contains a hub on one end, a spigot on the other. In between is the "barrel." While special tools are required, you can rent a calking iron, ladle, lead pot and furnace. Or you can use a propane torch instead of a plumbers furnace. Joining hub and spigot requires positioning both parts as shown. Oakum calking is packed in using a calking iron and hammer. Wearing asbestos gloves, heat ladle while you melt lead. Take a full dipper of hot lead and fill joint. Try to do it in one pouring. When lead cools, drive lead down around pipe using the calking iron.

If you don't want to use hub and spigot, use no-hub cast iron, Illus. 27; or cast iron compression gaskets, Illus. 28.

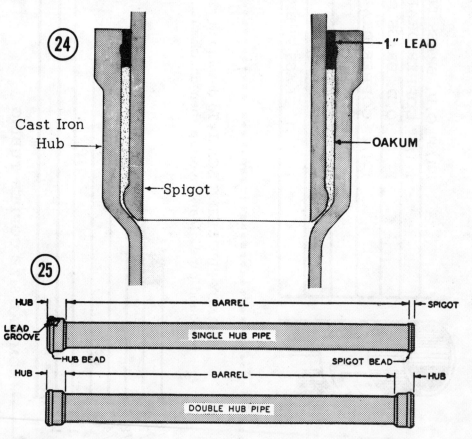

24

1" LEAD

Cast Iron
Hub

OAKUM

Spigot

25

HUB    BARREL    SPIGOT

LEAD
GROOVE    SINGLE HUB PIPE

HUB BEAD    SPIGOT BEAD

HUB    BARREL    HUB

DOUBLE HUB PIPE

**Plumbers' Ladle**

Calking
Iron

(26)

Lead
Pot

Plumbers
Furnace

No-Hub cast iron

(27)

neoprene gasket

stainless steel
clamp

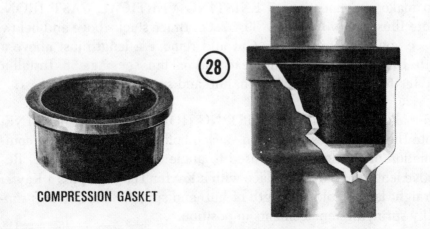

(28)

COMPRESSION GASKET

No-hub cast iron pipe and fittings are available in the same assortment and same sizes as hub and spigot cast iron. All you do is cut pipe to length required, slip a neoprene gasket in position, Illus. 29. Slip the stainless steel collar in position. The fitting or pipe to be joined, is inserted in gasket, bolts on collar tightened, and you have a joint that will last as long as cast iron or stainless steel, Illus. 30.

Besides being easy-to-join, it's remarkably quiet. The neoprene gasket tends to deaden noise immeasurably.

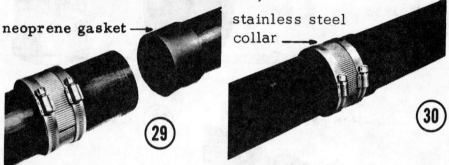

neoprene gasket →

stainless steel collar →

(29)  (30)

Illus. 25 shows two lengths of 4″ cast iron hub pipe. Both come in 5′ and 10′ lengths. One is called single hub, the other double hub. The outlet end of single hub pipe is called a spigot. If you have to cut a length of hub pipe, always use pipe with double hubs. This permits using both pieces. Connecting hub and spigot, or hub to a cut, or plain end, requires oakum calking and hot lead, Illus. 24. Note directions on page 57.

To make a connection to EXISTING VERTICAL CAST IRON. Note Illus. 4, 31, 32, 36, 38, 39, 57, 68. Brace stack above and below piece you want to remove.[1] Cut and remove a length just above a hub, Illus. 75. Remove stub, lead and oakum, see page 58. Install a kayfer tee and straight length, hub and spigot, page 60.

To make a connection to EXISTING HORIZONTAL SOIL LINE, note Illus. 31, pages 32, 39. An ⅛ Bend offset, Illus. 31, or any combination of fittings, can be used to angle over to existing line. Remove length of barrel, replace with a Kayfer Tee or Y, plus a Kayfer straight length, plus a length of hub and spigot. Three fittings simplify springing replacements in position.

[1]See page 118.

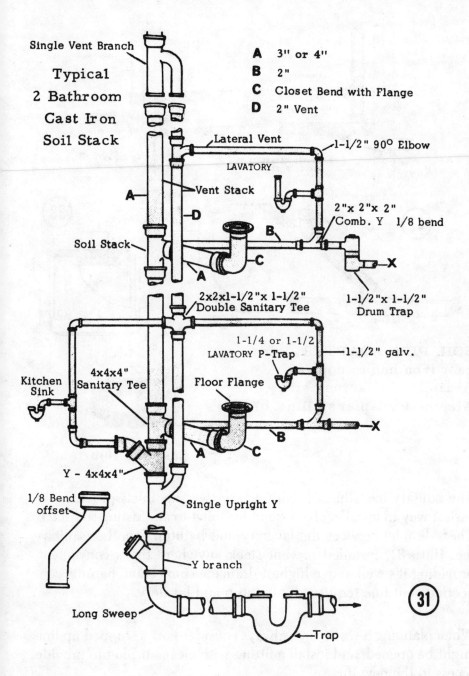

**Typical 2 Bathroom Cast Iron Soil Stack**

Single Vent Branch

A — 3" or 4"
B — 2"
C — Closet Bend with Flange
D — 2" Vent

Lateral Vent

1-1/2" 90° Elbow

LAVATORY

Vent Stack

A

D

2"x 2"x 2" Comb. Y 1/8 bend

Soil Stack

B

X

C

A

1-1/2"x 1-1/2" Drum Trap

2x2x1-1/2"x 1-1/2" Double Sanitary Tee

1-1/4 or 1-1/2 LAVATORY P-Trap

1-1/2" galv.

Kitchen Sink

4x4x4" Sanitary Tee

Floor Flange

X

A

B

C

Y – 4x4x4"

1/8 Bend offset

Single Upright Y

Y branch

Long Sweep

Trap

31

Or you can run a 3″ line directly to sewer line in basement. Here a connection can frequently be made by removing a cleanout plug and threaded ferrule, Illus. 32, 33, adding a soil pipe adapter, Illus. 33A. This connects cast iron hub to copper waste line.

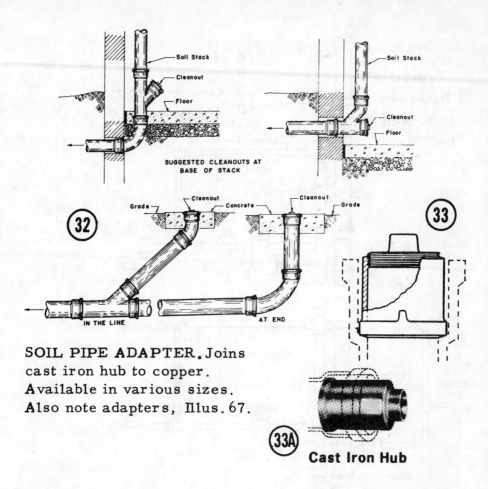

**32**

SUGGESTED CLEANOUTS AT
BASE OF STACK

Soil Stack
Cleanout
Floor

Soil Stack
Cleanout
Floor

Grade — Cleanout — Concrete — Cleanout — Grade

IN THE LINE

AT END

**33**

SOIL PIPE ADAPTER. Joins
cast iron hub to copper.
Available in various sizes.
Also note adapters, Illus. 67.

**33A**

**Cast Iron Hub**

The sanitary tee, Illus. 31, with one or two side inlets provides the easiest way to install a closet bend for toilet to an existing soil stack. The side inlet services the lavatory and bathtub. Another sanitary tee, Illus. 31, installed in vent stack anywhere that's convenient, providing it's well above highest drainage connection, permits connecting vent line required by bathtub and lavatory.

When planning a waste line, always consider how a stopped up line might be opened, and install a fitting with cleanout plug to provide access to the new line.

To remove a rusted cleanout plug, apply Liquid Wrench or equal to threads, tap plug with hammer and unscrew plug. Stuff a wet rag in opening. Apply torch to hub, melt the lead, remove ferrule with pliers. Or you can use a cold chisel and hammer to remove ferrule. Always stuff a wet rag in opening before applying heat or before using a cold chisel. Remove all lead and oakum. Be sure to insulate wall around fitting with a piece of sheet asbestos, or sheet aluminum before applying torch.

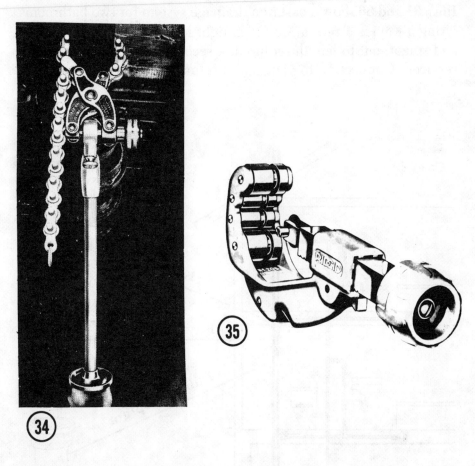

The cast iron pipe cutter, Illus. 34, and copper tubing cutter, Illus. 35, are real work savers and can be rented for time needed,

You can cut cast iron with a cold chisel and a hammer; cut copper tubing with a hacksaw, and melt lead in a solder bucket using a propane torch.

Study each illustration and note words used to describe various parts of a plumbing system. Note also how differently a bathtub, lavatory and toilet can be vented, how each works perfectly when installed as illustrated. Your plumber, and/or building or plumbing inspector, will recommend venting that local codes require, and can draw a sketch for you.

Illus. 31 and 36 show a cast iron drainage system for two bathrooms. Using a Kayfer T plus a Kayfer straight length and a length of hub and spigot, cut to length required, a second floor bathroom can be serviced. Connection to vent lines are made where convenient.

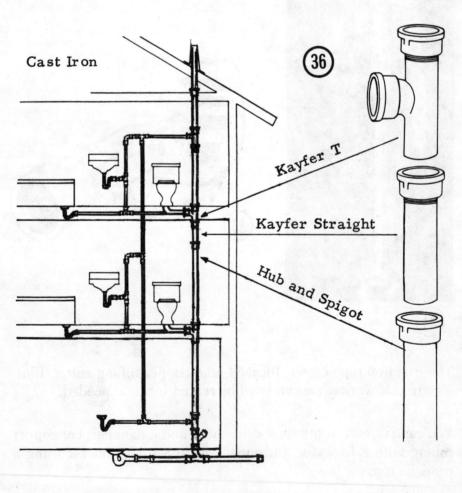

Cast Iron

(36)

Kayfer T

Kayfer Straight

Hub and Spigot

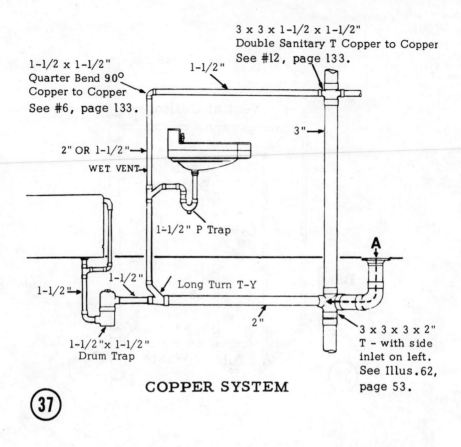

1-1/2 x 1-1/2"
Quarter Bend 90°
Copper to Copper
See #6, page 133.

1-1/2"

3 x 3 x 1-1/2 x 1-1/2"
Double Sanitary T Copper to Copper
See #12, page 133.

3"

2" OR 1-1/2"
WET VENT

1-1/2" P Trap

A

1-1/2"

1-1/2"

Long Turn T-Y

1-1/2"x 1-1/2"
Drum Trap

2"

3 x 3 x 3 x 2"
T - with side
inlet on left.
See Illus.62,
page 53.

**COPPER SYSTEM**

(37)

Illus. 37 shows a 3″ copper soil stack, 2″ drainage, 1½″ vent line. The bathtub drains through 1½″ copper pipe to a drum trap, thence into 2″ copper. The lavatory drains into a 1½″ copper. In this type of installation the lavatory drain pipe acts as a wet vent, liquid and air flow through same pipe. While most codes allow a wet vent, some specify 2″ minimum. The toilet is connected to 3″ copper soil stack.

Illus. 38 shows a two bathroom, back-to-back installation. While most homes contain 4″ cast iron soil stack, 1½″ or 2″ galvanized iron vent and drainage lines, 3″ cast iron, copper and plastic can now be used instead of 4″. 1½″ and 2″ copper or plastic or 2″ no-hub cast iron is easier to install than galvanized iron. Galvanized requires too many tools.

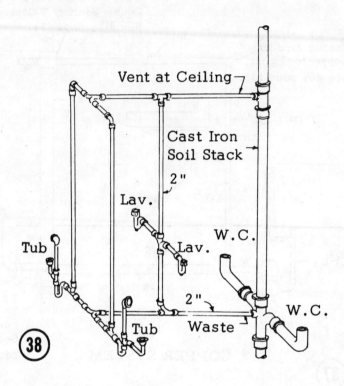

Illus. 39 shows another "typical" plumbing tree. Note method of venting toilet required by some codes.

Most codes allow a 4″ cast iron soil stack to accommodate up to six toilets. The soil stack is called a vent stack when it passes point where drainage enters line. Codes allow the soil stack to vent a toilet providing the lineal distance of A, Illus. 37, is not more than 36″, (some codes allow 72″). Distance A is figured from center of inlet opening in closet bend to center of soil stack, and is measured by following dotted line. Position toilet distance from soil stack codes specify, or vent it as shown in Illus. 39.

If location of toilet requires a separate soil stack, run a 3″ copper, plastic, or cast iron directly to sewer line in basement.

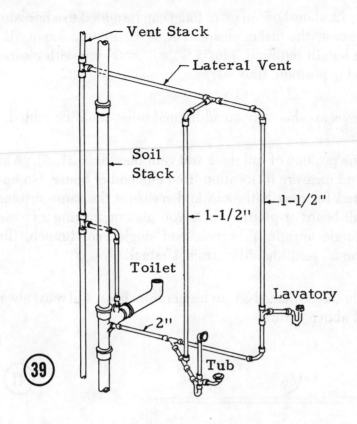

Vent Stack

Lateral Vent

Soil
Stack

1-1/2"

1-1/2"

Toilet

Lavatory

2"

Tub

(39)

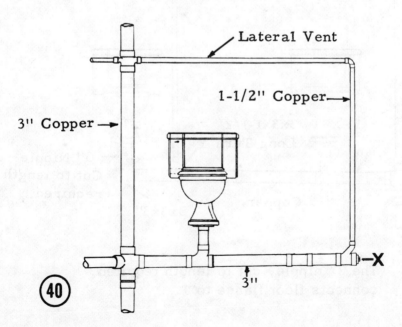

Lateral Vent

1-1/2" Copper

3" Copper

X

3"

(40)

Illus. 40, 41, 42, show how an extra toilet can be added to a horizontal line. In this case, the fitting cleanout X, Illus. 40, was removed, 3″ tube cut to length required, plus a 3″ x 3″ x 3″ tee with cleanout was sweated in position, Illus. 41.

Illus. 42 shows another way an additional toilet could be added.

To determine position of soil stack and vent line, Illus. 31, 43, go into basement and measure its location from one end of house. Go up to room selected for new bathroom and measure the same distance. Remove wall board or plaster where you plan on making a connection. The single upright Y branch, and single vent branch, Illus. 31 places the 2″ vent line, 5½″ from 4″ stack.

Vent lines should be placed 36″ or higher from floor, and must always be installed above fixture.

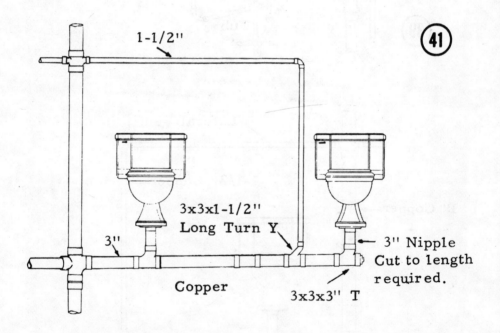

The 3″ nipple, cut to length required, connects floor flange to T.

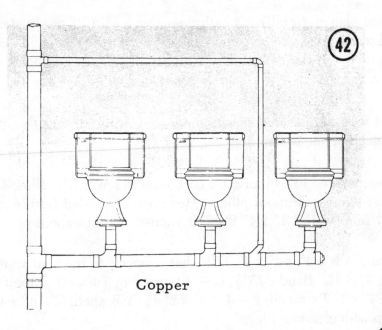

Copper

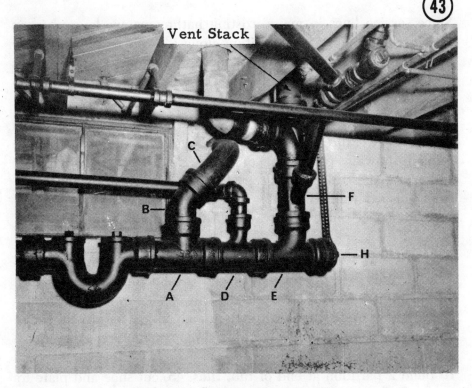

Vent Stack

Hub and Spigot Cast Iron

If you plan on installing a bathroom above existing one, water, vent and waste lines, can be run up against an existing wall and enclosed in a closet, or dummy wall, or wall can be opened and holes drilled through shoe.

Cast iron, copper and plastic have compatible fittings that permit connecting one to another.

If you wanted to add an extra bathroom to sewer line, Illus. 43, you could remove cleanout plug at H; remove threaded ferrule and install another 4" x 4" x 4" 90° T Branch-E  with cleanout plug H.

Fitting A is a 4" x 4" x 4" TEE that connects to fresh air vent; B — 4" x 4" x ⅛" Bend (45°); C — Extra Long Turn 90° Elbow; D — 4" x 4" x 2" T Branch; F — 4" x 4" x 2" 45° Y Branch; G — 4" x 4" x 4" Trap with cleanout plugs.

Since service lines in many existing bathrooms are located in an outside wall, building an addition alongside this wall offers many advantages. It not only provides more insulation for your present room, but also simplifies making connections. A ventilating fan provides needed circulation of air in an inside bathroom.

After one, two, three, or as many readings as you require, draw up a plan showing placement of fixtures, Illus. 1. Use template and grid, pages 121, 159. Be sure to indicate opening for toilet, 12" from finished wall, Illus. 44, or distance from wall manufacturer specifies; space toilet 15" away from side walls.

Ilus. 45 shows typical 2x4 framing required to partition off a bathroom. In this case the toilet is placed behind framing required at end of tub. A window was installed in outside wall. Since many codes now permit ventilating fans for an inside bathroom, frame opening for code approved fan following manufacturer's directions.

To build a partition at end of tub, Illus. 45, cut shoe and plate to width of tub less ⅝", or thickness of gypsum board used. This will

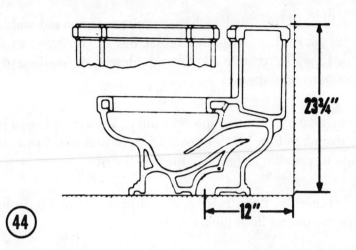

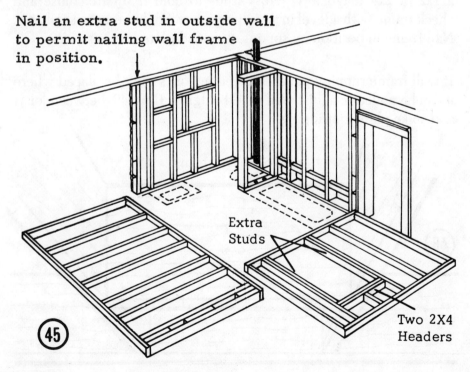

44

23¾"

12"

allow gypsum board to finish flush with tub. When end of partition is tiled the tile butts against tile on sides.

FRAMING. Draw lines on floor to indicate overall size of proposed bathroom. Finished flooring must be removed if you want mosaic tile in new bathroom to finish flush with adjoining floor.

Nail an extra stud in outside wall to permit nailing wall frame in position.

Extra Studs

45

Two 2X4 Headers

Remove wallboard from walls where required. If you cut wallboard along center of stud, it simplifies replacing. If you want to apply ceramic tile to walls, remove all existing plaster or wallboard and follow directions on page 75.

Since you will have to remove sub-flooring in any area where a closet bend and drainage line is to be installed, cut and nail 2x4 cats between joists to provide a shoulder for sub-flooring.

Build wall frames on floor, raise and nail in position. Try to locate one wall frame over a floor joist.

Before measuring lumber for length, check end with a square. Cut shoe and plate to length required. Measure height of room at both ends of a frame. Cut studs to length required. Spike shoe and plate to end studs with two 16 penny nails to each joint. Space and nail studs 16″ on center. Check frame for square by measuring diagonals. When diagonals are equal length, frame is considered square. Nail a 1x2 or 2x4 diagonally across studs to hold it square. Raise and check frame with a level in two directions to make certain it's plumb. Nail frame in position by spiking shoe and plate into joists.

If wall frame running parallel to ceiling joists can't be placed where it can be nailed to a joist, nail solid bridging, Illus. 46, between joists and spike plate to bridging.

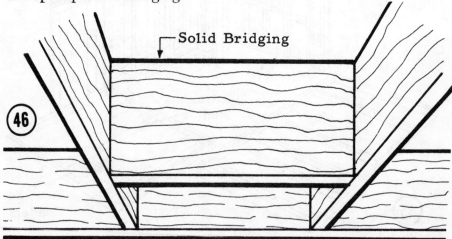

Solid Bridging

46

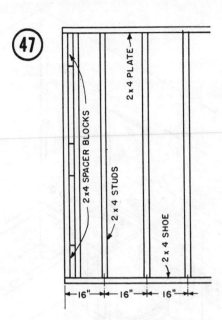

To provide backing at corners for gypsum wallboard, nail extra 2x4 spacer blocks and studs in position shown, Illus. 47, in corners.

Frame opening for door to rough opening size door frame requires. Most bathroom doors are 2'6" x 6'8". Use double 2x4 header over door, single jack studs under header as shown, Illus. 45.

Illus. 48 shows suggested height for various bathroom fixtures.

If bathtub manufacturer specifies nailing a 2x4 horizontally across studs, to support edge of tub against wall, install same following directions supplied with fixture.

The bathtub, diverter valve, shower head, tub spout, lavatory, and shower curtain rod sockets require backing boards. Some grab and towel bars require backing boards, while others are cemented in position with special adhesives sold at ceramic tile counters. Some soap trays and toilet paper receptacles are installed with adhesives. A medicine chest, window, heater and/or fan, require 2x4 cats. Always frame rough opening to size product manufacturer specifies.

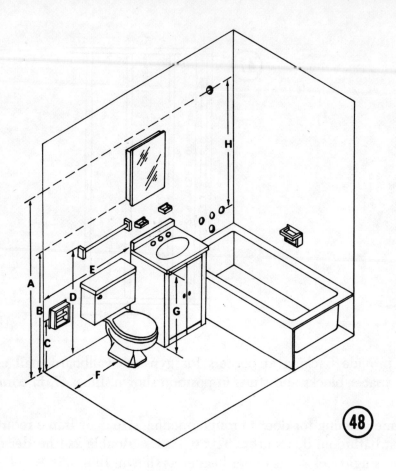

(48)

A - 6'6" Shower Head Elbow
B - 48" to 52" Medicine Chest
C - 30" to 35" Paper Holder
D - 42" Towel Bar
E - 30" min. Toilet Spacing
F - 15" min. Toilet Spacing
G - 31" approx. Lavatory
H - 52-1/2" suggested Diverter Valve
   **Tub Spout 4-1/2" below Diverter Valve**
   Shower Curtain 78"  } **from floor**
   Bag Hook 60" to 66"  }
   Grab Bar - optional

To provide backing for diverter valve and tub spout, nail a 1x8 to studs in position indicated, Illus. 49. 2x4's nailed in position shown, provide support for shower supply lines, Illus. 50.

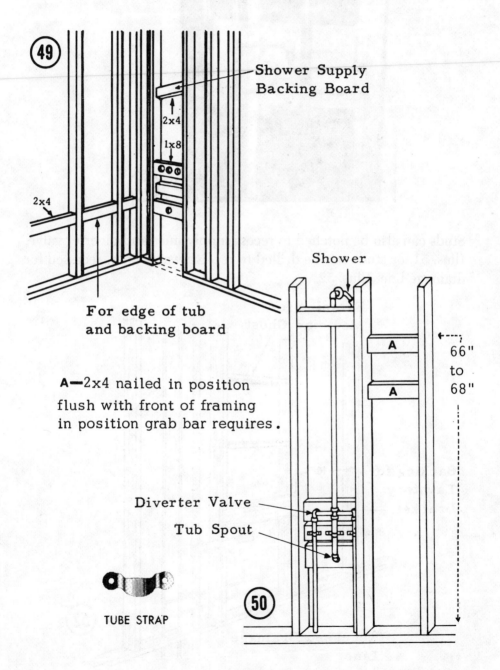

Shower Supply
Backing Board

2x4

1x8

2x4

For edge of tub
and backing board

Shower

A—2x4 nailed in position
flush with front of framing
in position grab bar requires.

A

A

66"
to
68"

Diverter Valve

Tub Spout

TUBE STRAP

Diverter Valve

Tub Spout

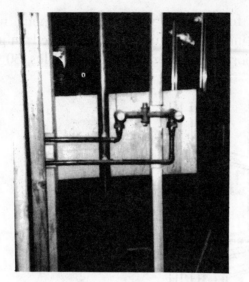

(51)

Studs can also be notched to recess supply lines and diverter valve, Illus. 51, or studs can be drilled to receive water lines, recessed for drainage line, Illus. 52.

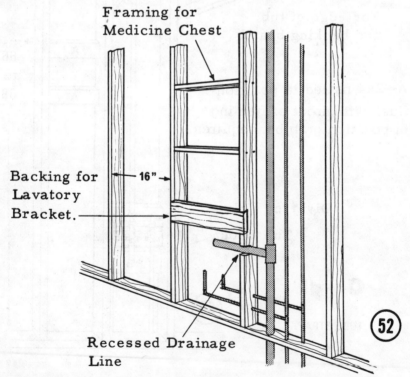

Framing for
Medicine Chest

Backing for
Lavatory
Bracket.

◄ 16" ►

Recessed Drainage
Line

(52)

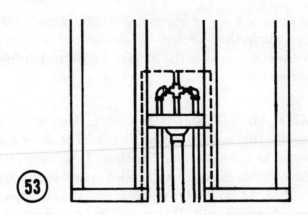

(53)

Dash lines, Illus. 53, indicate position of removable inspection panel recommended on wall backing up against drum trap connection to bathtub. This permits inspecting and servicing trap. Use ⅛" hardboard or ¼" plywood. Screw or hinge to studs.

Visualizing direction, pitch, and fittings required to run a 3" or 4" waste line to sewer connection can be simplified by using a six foot folding rule and a 1x2 by length needed. If you need more help, try stiffening a garden hose with wire cut from coat hangers. After cutting and straightening hangers, tape wire to outside of hose, Illus. 54. After setting closet bend and tee in position, Illus. 55, tie hose to outlet end of tee, run hose to sewer connection. Make bends in hose comparable to fittings noted on pages 132 through 155.

NOTE: The author has purposely repeated certain step-by-step instructions to alert the reader to their importance

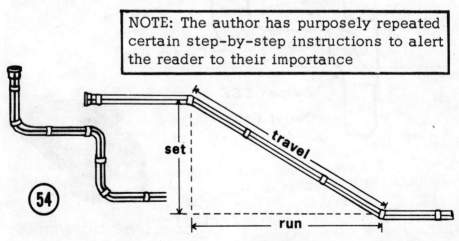

(54)    set    travel    run

The slope of a sewer line is important. It can be vertical or any horizontal angle that pitches ¼" or more to a foot. This visualization provides an idea as to the length of pipe and fittings your installation requires.

FACTS ABOUT ROUGHING-IN. The waste outlet in a toilet, Illus. 55, connects to a floor flange. The floor flange is sweated or screwed to a closet bend. The closet bend must, therefore, be placed distance from finished wall toilet manufacturer specifies. We show 12", Illus. 44, to center of opening. The distance is always figured from a finished wall. If you nail ⅝" vinyl faced gypsum board to studs, and apply ceramic tile, you would measure over 13" from studs.

If possible, position closet bend, Illus. 55, so it is placed parallel to floor joists. Always try to center closet bend between floor joists. Knock out bridging if necessary. If you need to place toilet close to a joist, use an offset closet fitting, Illus. 56.

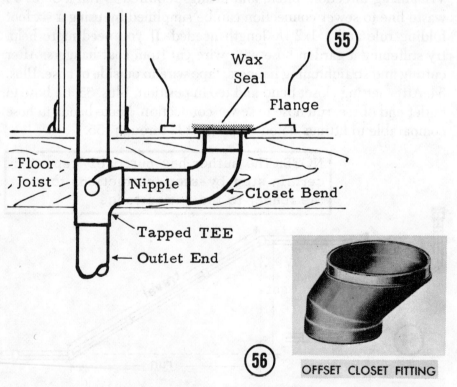

55

Wax
Seal

Flange

- Floor
, Joist

Nipple

Closet Bend′

Tapped TEE

← Outlet End

56

OFFSET CLOSET FITTING

An offset closet bend, Illus. 56, permits placing toilet close to, even over a joist without cutting away too much joist.

If closet bend is placed at right angle to floor joists, use a short length of pipe — A, Illus. 57, to connect to closet bend. This permits dropping bend down below floor joists. This presents no problem in a first floor installation with unfinished basement below. If room below has a finished ceiling, 3″ pipe can be run through holes sawed in floor joists, Illus. 58.

Cast iron closet bends can be screwed to floor flange, Illus. 57. Others available can be calked with oakum and lead.

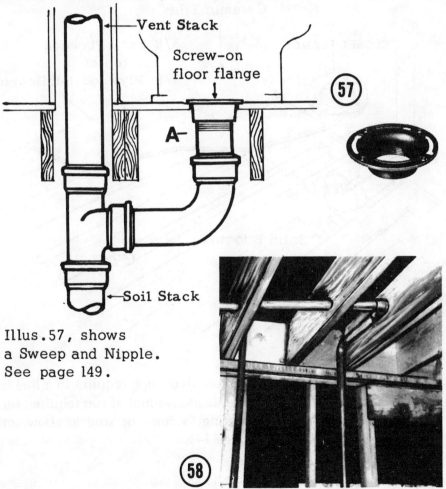

Illus. 57, shows
a Sweep and Nipple.
See page 149.

Another way of making an installation without disturbing a ceiling below is by raising the floor, Illus. 59. Use 2x4, 2x6 or size joists required. While this necessitates a step up into new bathroom, it does simplify roughing-in. Solid bridging, lumber of same dimension as floor joists, nailed in position shown, reinforces joists that have been notched or drilled.

If you have to run a line across a room, it can be enclosed with a storage wall[1], partition, or supported with plumbing straps or brackets, Illus. 60. Always brace an existing line above and below area to be cut. See Page 118.

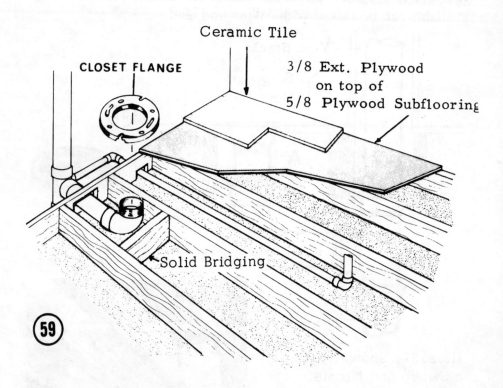

Ceramic Tile

CLOSET FLANGE

3/8 Ext. Plywood on top of 5/8 Plywood Subflooring

Solid Bridging

(59)

The amount of space a fitting or length of pipe requires in a line is called "the run". Pages 142-155 indicate amount of run required for fittings illustrated. When estimating "a run", be sure to allow for space pipe goes into a fitting, page 141.

[1]See Book L34-634, How to Build Wall to Wall Storage Units.

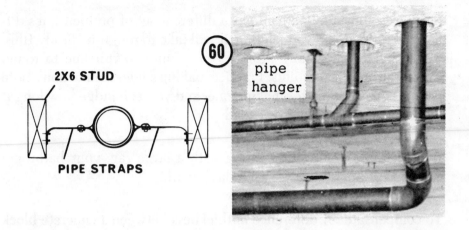

**2X6 STUD**

**PIPE STRAPS**

⑥⓪

pipe
hanger

Complete kits containing fittings required for waste and vent installations are now available in cast iron, copper and plastic, Illus. 61, from plumbing supply retailers.

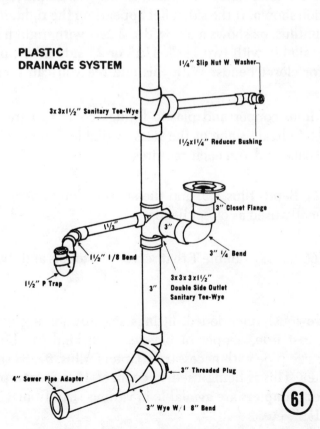

**PLASTIC DRAINAGE SYSTEM**

1¼" Slip Nut W Washer

3 x 3 x 1½" Sanitary Tee-Wye

1½ x 1¼" Reducer Bushing

3" Closet Flange

1½"

3"

1½" 1/8 Bend

3" ¼ Bend

1½" P Trap

3 x 3 x 3 x 1½"
Double Side Outlet
Sanitary Tee-Wye

3"

4" Sewer Pipe Adapter

3" Threaded Plug

3" Wye W/ I 8" Bend

⑥①

Since every installation contains a different set of problems, it's difficult to estimate how much time it will take to rough-in. Study Illus. 31. Estimate how many fittings you require to run line to toilet. Count the number of joints. Practice making solder connections, note page 83. Check time for making one, and you can judge how long it will take to rough-in those needed.

By plugging opening in a fitting with a large rag, your bathroom can be kept operable after each day's work.

To compensate for difference in thickness between a concrete block wall and 2x4 wall framing, use a 1/8 bend offset, Illus. 31, also page 140.

Fittings are available with side inlets, Illus. 62; on one, or both sides. To determine what hand fitting you require, place fitting in position shown. If the side inlet appears on the right, it's a right hand fitting. Illus. 62 shows a 3 x 3 x 3 x 2 tee with right hand inlet. Tees are available with two 1¼", 1½" or 2" side inlets, plus two 3" inlets for closet bends. With this one tee you can serve two toilets.

Cast iron, copper and plastic fittings come in various sizes. Illus. 63, 64, indicate some of the sizes available. Pages 142 – 155 indicate space and run each requires.

The ¼ Bend, Illus. 65, and the short or long sweep, page 139, are frequently used as closet bends.

Illus. 66 shows a double T that serves two toilets and two 2 " branch lines.

As previously mentioned, fittings simplify joining various kinds of pipe, cast iron, copper or plastic. Each kind can be connected to other size pipe with necessary adapters. Illus. 67, 68 shows a 4" x 3" adapter. This is being used to connect 4" cast iron pipe hub to 3" copper. Adapters are available in various sizes from 4" x 3", 4" x 2", 4" x 1½", etc.

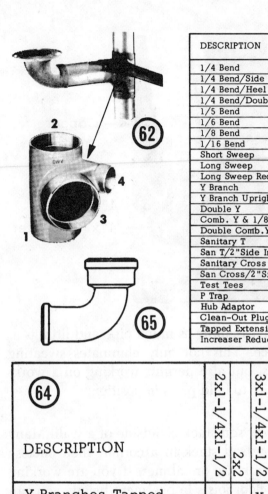

| DESCRIPTION | SIZE (INCHES) | | | | | | |
|---|---|---|---|---|---|---|---|
| | 2 | 3 | 4 | 3x2 | 3x4 | 4x2 | 4x3 |
| 1/4 Bend | x | x | x | | | | |
| 1/4 Bend/Side Inlet | | | | x | | x | |
| 1/4 Bend/Heel Inlet | | | | x | | x | |
| 1/4 Bend/Double | x | x | x | | | | |
| 1/5 Bend | x | x | x | | | | |
| 1/6 Bend | x | x | x | | | | |
| 1/8 Bend | x | x | x | | | | |
| 1/16 Bend | x | x | x | | | | |
| Short Sweep | x | x | x | | | | |
| Long Sweep | x | x | x | | | | |
| Long Sweep Reducing | | | | x | | | x |
| Y Branch | x | x | x | x | | x | x |
| Y Branch Upright | x | x | x | x | | x | x |
| Double Y | x | x | x | x | | x | x |
| Comb. Y & 1/8 Bend | x | x | x | x | | x | x |
| Double Comb.Y & 1/8 Bend | x | x | x | x | | x | x |
| Sanitary T | x | x | x | x | x | x | x |
| San T/2"Side Inlet | | x | x | | x | | x |
| Sanitary Cross | x | x | x | x | | x | x |
| San Cross/2"Side Inlet | | x | | | | | |
| Test Tees | x | x | x | | | | |
| P Trap | x | x | x | | | | |
| Hub Adaptor | x | x | x | | | | |
| Clean-Out Plug | x | x | x | | | | |
| Tapped Extension Piece | x | x | | | | | |
| Increaser Reducer | | | | x | x | x | |

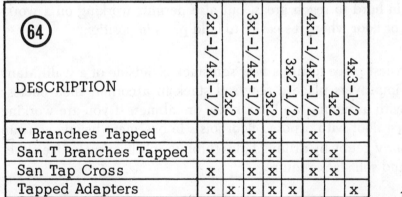

| DESCRIPTION | 2x1-1/4x1-1/2 | 2x2 | 3x1-1/4x1-1/2 | 3x2 | 3x2-1/2 | 4x1-1/4x1-1/2 | 4x2 | 4x3-1/2 |
|---|---|---|---|---|---|---|---|---|
| Y Branches Tapped | | | x | x | | x | | |
| San T Branches Tapped | x | x | x | x | | x | x | |
| San Tap Cross | x | | x | x | | x | x | |
| Tapped Adapters | x | x | x | x | x | | | x |

1-1/2"

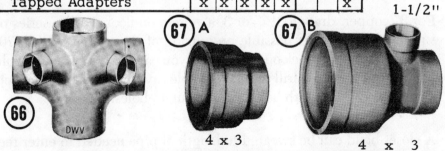

4 x 3          4 x 3

67A-SOIL PIPE ADAPTER, joins cast iron hub to
    copper. 4"x3", 4"x2", 4"x1-1/2", plus other sizes.
67B-Joins CI hub to 3" copper to 1-1/2" copper.

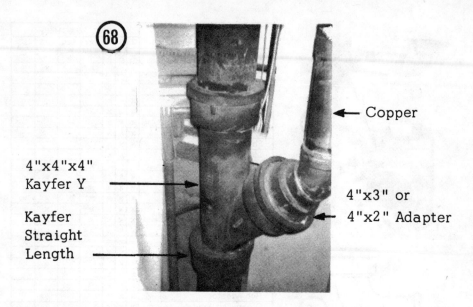

(68)

4"x4"x4"
Kayfer Y ———→

Kayfer
Straight
Length ————→

Copper ◄——

4"x3" or
4"x2" Adapter ◄——

To rough-in like a "pro", pre-assemble as much pipe and fittings as you can install in one piece. This not only eliminates sweating joints in hard to reach areas, but also permits working on a work-bench or floor where it's easier to hold parts in position.

The easiest place to run a new soil stack is outside of a wall. Many home improvers place a new soil stack in a corner, then enclose same with a dummy wall, bookcase or cabinet. If you are working on a first floor with exposed floor joists in basement below, you can frequently get by by drilling holes through sub-flooring to size closet bend and soil stack require.

For 3" copper, draw a 3¼" or 3⅜" circle on floor. Drill a series of ¼" holes as close as possible on outside of drawn lines, Illus. 70. Using a hammer, knock out center. Or you can use a high speed hole saw, Illus. 71. A ¼" drill will take a hole saw that cuts openings up to 1½"; a ½" drill with hole saw will cut 4" holes.

A closet bend can be sweated to length of pipe needed to enter tee, then sweated to tee, Illus. 55, or you can use a long tangent closet bend, Illus. 72. While these cost more, they eliminate need for a short nipple.

54

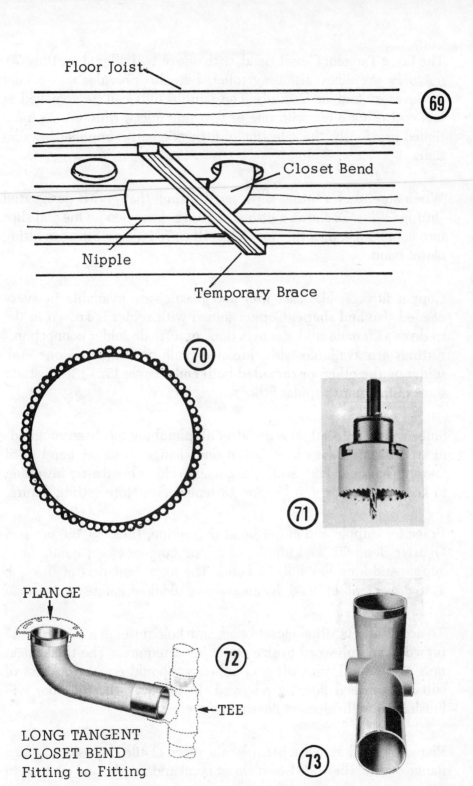

Floor Joist

69

Closet Bend

Nipple

Temporary Brace

70

71

FLANGE

72

TEE

LONG TANGENT
CLOSET BEND
Fitting to Fitting

73

The Long Tangent Closet Bend, with one or two side inlets, Illus. 73, not only simplifies installing toilet, but also provides waste inlet for lavatory and/or bathtub. The same results can be achieved at less cost using a tee with one or two side inlets, Illus. 62. As mentioned previously, the selection of fittings greatly simplifies installation.

When an end of a fitting slips into a fitting, that end is designated "fitting." Illus. 72 shows a fitting to fitting closet bend. One end slips into floor flange, the other into a tee. Illus. 73 is also a fitting to fitting closet bend.

Copper fittings, like cast iron and plastic, are available in every needed size and shape. Copper joined with solder is known in the trade as a "female solder connection" or a "male solder connection." Fittings are available with threaded male or female on one end, solder on the other, or threaded both ends. Pages 132 - 136 illustrate some of the more popular fittings.

Since you will install floor tile after all plumbing has been roughed-in, and bathtub set, don't fasten floor flange to closet bend until floor tile has been laid. Stuff a large rag in closet bend after installing to keep out debris, but be sure to remove it before setting fixture.

Brace tee, nipple and closet bend in position, Illus. 59, 69; or use a Quarter Bend 90° and nipple; or a long tangent closet bend, or a nipple and long low-hub ¼ bend. The important part of this job is to project closet bend distance above tile floor flange requires.

To accurately position closet bend, saw hole through a piece of ⅜" plywood and plyscord to size closet bend requires. The total thickness of plywood, plus tile and adhesive, should equal thickness of sub and finished flooring removed. In this way the tile floor will finish flush with adjacent flooring.

Place plywood across joists, place a piece of tile in position, place flange on tile, Illus. 74. Insert closet bend and nipple, and connect to

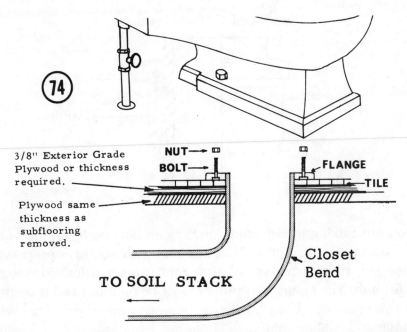

74

3/8" Exterior Grade
Plywood or thickness
required.

NUT→ ☐

BOLT→

☐

FLANGE

TILE

Plywood same
thickness as
subflooring
removed.

TO SOIL STACK

Closet
Bend

tee. Brace each fitting in position, but do not sweat. You can now dummy up soil line from tee to sewer connection or from sewer connection to tee. In either case, dummy up entire assembly, fittings and pipe in position to make sure everything fits. Hold parts in place with wire nailed to floor joists. When it's completely assembled and closet bend projects distance required, start sweating fittings and pipe. Pre-assemble as much as possible. Raise and brace in position. Connect to sewer and to tee, but do not connect to floor flange. When closet bend is in exact position flange requires, brace entire line with pipe strap.

## HOW TO JOIN HUB AND SPIGOT

If codes require cast iron hub and spigot pipe, it must be braced in position required before attempting to join. Oakum calking is driven in position shown with a calking iron and hammer, Illus. 75, to within 1" from top of hub. Hot lead is then poured into joint. Be sure to heat the ladle before dipping into hot lead. Wear asbestos gloves. Pour joint in one pouring. A full ladle of lead will usually fill a joint. After lead cools, use calking iron and hammer to drive lead ring firmly into hub around pipe. This produces a really tight, trouble free connection.

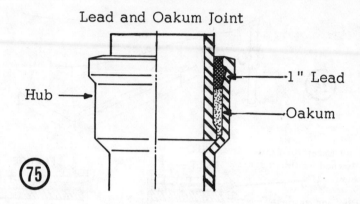

Lead and Oakum Joint

Hub →

1" Lead

Oakum

75

If you are calking a horizontal joint, again be sure to position and brace both parts in exact center. Pack joint with oakum as previously mentioned, then fasten an asbestos joint runner, Illus. 76, snugly against hub. The opening in runner must be on top. Lead is poured into this opening. When lead cools, remove runner, calk lead with hammer and calking iron.

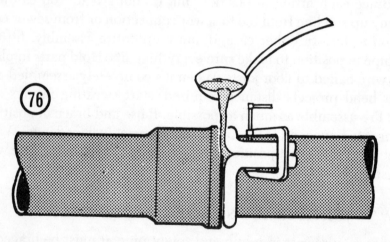

76

An easier type of cast iron to install, one now approved by most codes, is the compression joint. This is made with a neoprene compression gasket, Illus. 77. The gasket is inserted in hub. The spigot, or plain end of connecting pipe, or fitting, is forced in. This results in a superb compression joint in seconds. No oakum, no lead, no experience required. Your plumbing supply retailer will rent you a clamp that simplifies joining pipe and fittings in compression joints.

58

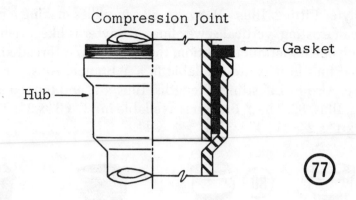

Compression Joint

Gasket

Hub

77

The no-hub cast iron, Illus. 78 comes in 5' and 10' lengths. Matching fittings are available that permit using this pipe wherever 2", 3" or 4" cast iron is required.

Cast iron soil pipe comes in two grades, XH — Extra Heavy and SV — Service.

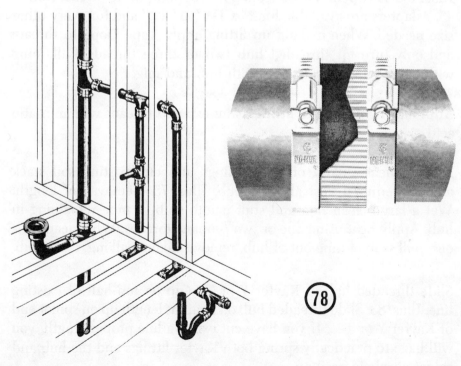

78

The Kayfer Fitting, Illus. 79, 80, 81, 82, simplifies making a connection to an existing, vertical sewer line. A Kayfer is like a regular fitting with one important exception; the hub at top is threaded. These threaded hub fittings are available in a Y branch, Illus. 79; or tee, Illus. 80. Also in 12" straight lengths, Illus. 81; and tapped straight lengths, Illus. 82. The Y Branch is available in: 3" x 3" x 2"; 3" x 3" x 3"; 4" x 4" x 2"; 4" x 4" x 3"; 4" x 4" x 4".

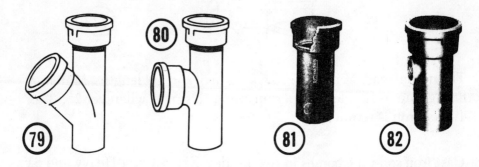

Illus. 68 shows a 4" x 4" x 4" Kayfer Y fitting with a 4" x 3" copper adapter, installed over a straight Kayfer. Note 4" x 3" copper adapter, Illus. 67. This permits connecting 3" copper, plastic or cast iron to 4". Adapters are available for 2" x 1½", 3" x 2" and for every other size needed. When making up fitting, apply Tape Dope to threads and only turn up threaded hub two or three threads. Calk joint with oakum and hot lead as with hub and spigot.

After making up Kayfer fitting, paint exposed threads with muriatic acid.

Always measure run of both fittings and cut existing soil stack amount required, just above a hub, Illus. 75. Remove cut length. Wet a large clean rag, and stuff it into stub of pipe remaining in hub. Apply heat using one or two propane torches. When lead softens, pull stub of pipe out of hub, remove oakum calking, clean hub.

Slide threaded hub of Kayfer Y or Tee up on top half of existing line, Illus. 83. Slide threaded hub on straight length up on spigot end of Kayfer Y or Tee. If you have cut existing line proper length, you will have to practically spring both Kayfer fittings and the hub and spigot nipple in position.

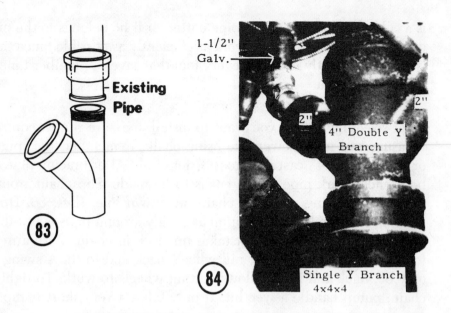

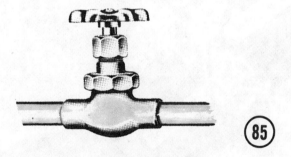

Illus. 84 shows how a double Y, 4″ x 4″ x 2″ x 2″ was installed over a 4″ x 4″ x 4″ single Kayfer Y and short length of hub and spigot.

Before starting work, flush toilet, shut off master valve, Illus. 85. alongside your water meter, switch off hot water heater. Open all faucets and drain water line at your lowest faucet. Put up "Please Do Not Use" signs in bathroom and kitchen.

The soil pipe cutter, Illus. 34, 86, is an important time and labor saver. While you can cut cast iron with a cold chisel and hammer, the soil pipe cutter does it easily and quickly. Available on a rental basis, this remarkable tool makes clean cuts in 4″ cast iron quicker than you can read this page. If you hire a plumber, find out whether he is a cold chisel and hammer pipe cutter, or if he belongs to the progressive school that tries to work as efficiently as possible. Since time is your most costly expense, every tool that saves a plumber time is important to you.

After selecting fittings you want to install, measure run it requires. Measure and mark sewer line using chalk. Remember, the spigot, or plain end of 4″ cast iron goes 3″ into hub. After bracing pipe on both ends, mark pipe where cut is to be made. Slip chain around pipe, with cutting wheel in chain on drawn line, Illus. 86. Hook chain over chain hook in position as snugly around pipe as possible. Turn adjusting knob, until it takes up slack in chain. With arm of tool at right angle to pipe, roll wheels back and forth. A swing of only 6″, back and forth, allows cutting wheels to work. To tighten chain, pump handle a wee bit. It only takes a very short pump to

take up slack in chain. If chain is too tight, you can't roll cutters. Don't force cutters to dig too deep. Easy does it. Continue rolling chain back and forth and a clean cut is made in minutes.

If you have to cut pipe using a hacksaw or cold chisel and hammer, make a pipe marker, Illus. 87. Cut a piece of aluminum or copper flashing about 1″ wide by length required. Be sure edge is true. Bend to shape shown. Place guide snugly around pipe. Using chalk or white pencil, mark pipe all the way around. This helps making a square cut.

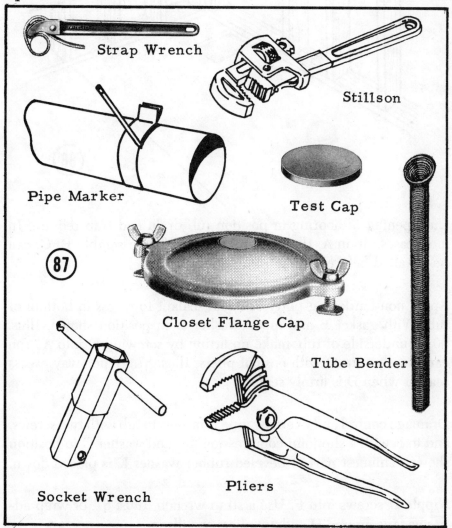

Strap Wrench

Stillson

Pipe Marker

Test Cap

87

Closet Flange Cap

Tube Bender

Socket Wrench

Pliers

BATHTUB INSTALLATION. After closet bend has been connected to sewer line and vent stack, drainage and vent lines for bathtub and lavatory roughed-in, nail plyscord to joists every 6" using 6 penny flooring or common nails. Use thickness that equals subflooring previously removed.

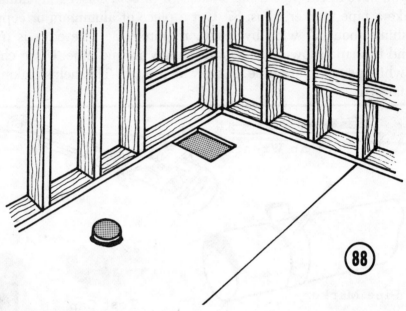

Cut opening in flooring in position tub drain and trap require. In most cases, drain A, Illus. 89, 90; and overflow assembly EFG, can be installed before setting tub in position.

Apply non-hardening putty or equal sealant to recess in bottom of tub. With gasket B and metal washer C in position shown, Illus. 90 on underside of tub, make up fitting by screwing D into A. You can usually turn D with nose of pliers, Illus. 87. Wipe away excess sealant when D is firmly seated.

Drainage control and overflow pipe E fastens to tub with two screws, and to F with a slip joint compression nut and washer G in position shown. Thinnest part of beveled rubber washer K is placed down.

Nipple H screws into F. Use a strap wrench, Illus. 87, or wrap adhesive tape around H and use pliers or stillson.

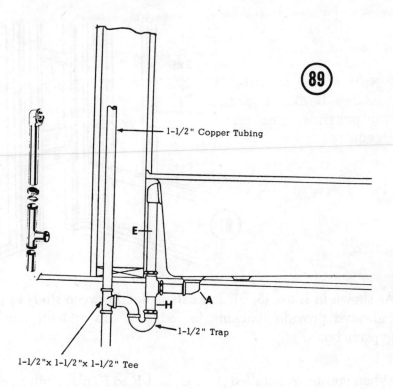

89

1-1/2" Copper Tubing

E

A

H

1-1/2" Trap

1-1/2"x 1-1/2"x 1-1/2" Tee

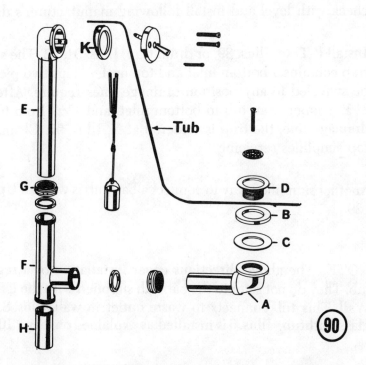

K

E

Tub

G

D

B

F

C

A

H

90

Nail studs to 2x6 or 2x8 backer board in position grab bar requires.

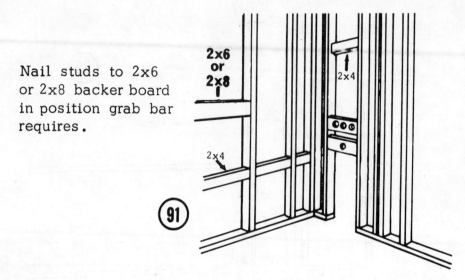

As shown in Illus. 45, 91, 2x4 cats nailed between studs in position indicated provide  backing for edge of tub and for vinyl faced gypsum board.

When you have installed A to D, and E to F, place tub in position check with level and install following manufacturer's directions.

Install P-Trap, Illus. 89, or drum trap, Illus. 31, 92. The swivel drum trap contains a bottom inlet and top outlet. This two piece trap can be swiveled to any position drainage lines require. After sweating 1½″ copper from tub to bottom inlet, and 1½″ from top outlet to drainage line, the trap is soldered at X, Illus. 92. Cleanout plug at top simplifies servicing.

Another simplified way to connect a bathtub is with an Upturn, Illus. 129.

NOTE: The above directions cover installation of a regular bathtub. They do not refer to the bathtub supplied with the EB Plumbing Wall. This tub connects to waste outlet in wall, Illus. 8. The fiber glass bathtub, Illus. 6 is installed as explained on page 100.

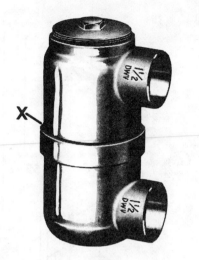

X

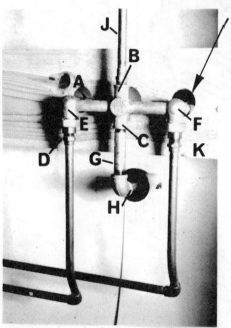

J

B

A

E

D

G

C

F

K

H

Drill 2" holes in backerboard
in position Diverter Valve
requires.

A– Diverter Valve
B– Shower Outlet
C– Tub Outlet
D– Male Adapter
E– Cold
F– Hot
G– Brass Nipple
H– Brass Ell
J– Shower Line
K–Female Coupling

Most bathtub manufacturers supply a three valve diverter unit, Illus. 93. This unit has two inlets, a cold on right, hot on left. Two outlets, one to shower, one to tub. Three controls, cold, hot and shower.

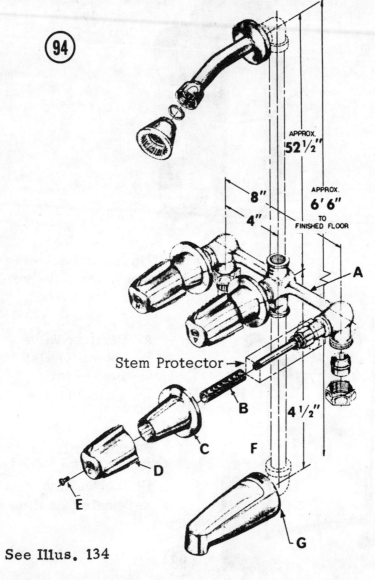

**94**

APPROX.
**52½″**

APPROX.
**6′ 6″**
TO
FINISHED FLOOR

8″

4″

A

Stem Protector →

B

C

D

E

F

4½″

G

**See Illus. 134**

Place diverter valve distance from finished wall manufacturer specifies. This is important for servicing.

½″ copper water lines are run to height fixture manufacturer recommends, or to height shown. Water lines for bathtub connect to a diverter valve, Illus. 94. The EB Plumbing Wall also provides this control valve.

To provide backing for edge of tub and vinyl covered gypsum board, nail 2x4's in position noted, Illus. 49. Also note 1x8 backing nailed to studs for diverter valve and tub spout. 2x4 nailed flush with back edge of studs provides support for shower supply line, Illus. 50. Using 2x4's frame in opening for an electric heater, built-in clothes hamper, radiator, etc.

A ½″ copper adapter with ½″ threaded male, Illus. 95, trade term: copper to M.S.P.S. (male standard pipe size) is sweated to ends of hot and cold water line, also to shower line, Illus. 93. The diverter valve is placed in position shown, Illus. 93, 94. The ½″ threaded male adapter screws into female coupling supplied with diverter valve. Fasten tubing to framing with tube straps, Illus. 50.

Keep stem protectors, Illus. 94, shipped with diverter, on stems until after tiling has been completed.

The ½″ copper shower supply line, Illus. 94, is cut to length required to place shower fitting 6′6″ from floor. Height of shower is optional.

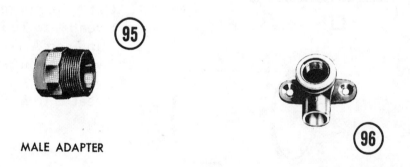

MALE ADAPTER

The ½″ x ½″ 90° Drop Ear Elbow, Illus. 96 is sweated to top of shower line. Screw shower line into diverter valve. Fasten line to backing with tube straps, Illus. 50. Insert a ½″ x 6″ threaded galvanized nipple into Drop Ear Elbow. After tiling has been completed, remove galvanized nipple, apply Tape Dope to threads and screw ½″ chrome nipple, supplied by fixture manufacturer, into elbow. Use a pipe strap wrench, or adhesive tape and pliers.

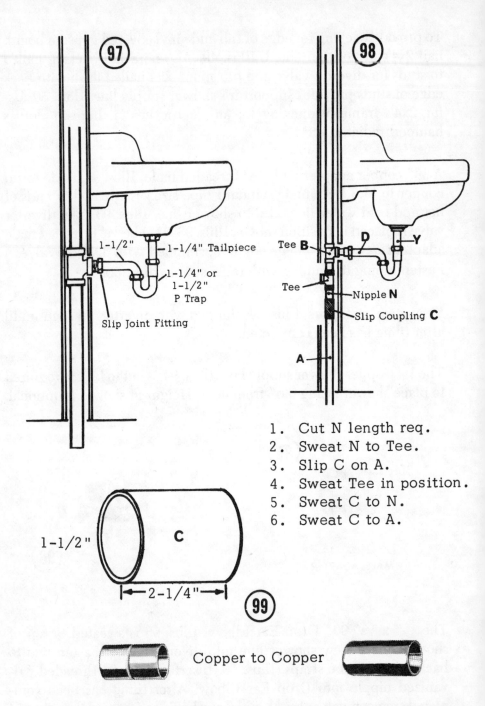

**97**

1-1/2"  1-1/4" Tailpiece

1-1/4" or
1-1/2"
P Trap

Slip Joint Fitting

**98**

Tee **B**  **D**  **Y**

Tee  Nipple **N**

Slip Coupling **C**

**A**

1. Cut N length req.
2. Sweat N to Tee.
3. Slip C on A.
4. Sweat Tee in position.
5. Sweat C to N.
6. Sweat C to A.

1-1/2"  **C**

← 2-1/4" →

**99**

Copper to Copper

COUPLING WITH STOP

COUPLING WITHOUT STOP

Illus. 94 indicates type of bathtub controls supplied with the EB Plumbing Wall. The backing for diverter valve, nailed to framing at factory, places valve 52½" below shower head; the tub spout approximately 4½" below. Two brass nipples and one brass 90° elbow, provided with the EB Wall, simplify installing tub spout. These can be installed prior to tiling. Apply Tape Dope to threads, fasten elbow to 4" nipple, other end into tub outlet in valve. Fasten 6" nipple into elbow. After tiling is completed, the chrome tub spout is screwed on nipple.

Due to the many variations that normally exist in roughing-in, i.e., thickness of lumber or plaster, bulge in plasterboard, slope in floor or wall, always double check length of pipe or nipple. Make a dry run, place parts together without flux or sweating to see if overall dimension is what you need.

FACTS ABOUT LAVATORY INSTALLATION. Many lavatories contain a 1¼" drain and tailpiece, Illus. 97, that connects to a 1½" P Trap with a compression fitting. Actually this fitting is no more than a 1½" threaded nut with a 1¼" hole in top. A nylon or lead compression ring, compresses when nut is tightened to make a watertight joint. This is called a 1½" x 1¼" compression joint adapter. The P Trap empties into 1½" drainage line that is also connected to a slip joint compression fitting.

A connection to an existing lavatory drainage and vent line A, Illus. 98, can be made in several ways. The easiest is to cut line A about 2" and 8" below existing tee B. Use a tube cutter, Illus. 35, or pipe marker, Illus. 87, and a hacksaw. Cut nipple length required from piece of pipe removed. Install another tee and a slip coupling C, Illus. 99. A slip coupling has no stop. If necessary to extend connection outside of finished wall, cut a nipple to length required, Illus. 100. Sweat tee to nipple. Sweat a coupling with slip joint connection, Illus. 101, to nipple. This permits connecting chrome or brass pipe of fixture drain.

You can also use a trap tee, Illus. 102, or a regular tee with a fitting slip joint adapter, Illus. 103. In this case the adapter is sweated into tee. These alternates are mentioned because your retailer might be out of stock on one item and an unskilled sales clerk won't know about substitutes.

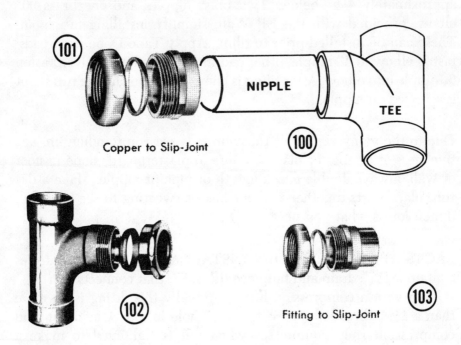

Copper to Slip-Joint

NIPPLE

TEE

Fitting to Slip-Joint

Prepare cut ends of A and fittings, apply Swif or equal solder. Sweat nipple to tee, slide C on A, sweat adapter, or nipple and adapter to tee before sweating tee to A.

Chrome waste line D, Illus. 98, slips into nut and lead washer in adapter. By tightening nut you compress washer.

Another way to make a connection to a waste, vent or water line is shown in Illus. 104. Disconnect line C by loosening compression nuts B. Cut line A just above tee and 6″ above. Apply heat and remove tee, nipple and/or slip joint adapter from tee. Prepare ends of line A for solder. Install a Double Long Turn T-Y, Illus. 105. While this fitting will project beyond most plasterboard walls, use a nipple if same is required. Join line with a slip coupling and nipple as shown, Illus. 106.

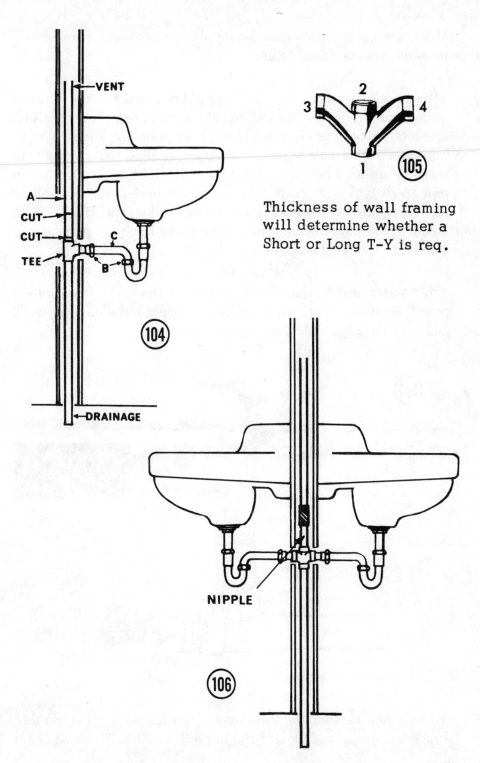

VENT

A

CUT

CUT

C

TEE

B

104

DRAINAGE

2

3          4

1          105

Thickness of wall framing
will determine whether a
Short or Long T-Y is req.

NIPPLE

106

73

Using a tee, slip coupling, and a nipple you can make a connection to water, vent or drainage line.

After installing waste, vent and supply lines, make a test. This requires temporarily plugging all openings with caps, Illus. 107. Both screw or sweat caps are available at your plumbing supply dealer. You can attach a male or female boiler drain, Illus. 108, anywhere to new line, attach a hose and watch for water or air leaks. Or you can rent an air tank with gauge. If it holds, you have done an excellent job. If it fails, use soap and water to find leaky joint. Heat joint to take it apart and remember to dry, clean, and prepare parts as you would any new connection.

A hot water heating line should be roughed-in while joists are exposed. Most baseboard radiation is now being installed after walls and floor have been tiled.

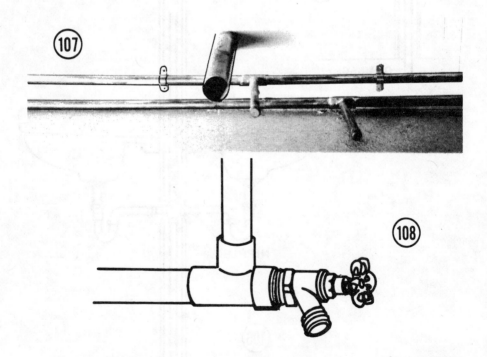

To keep new ceramic tile floor level with adjacent flooring, do this. Brace tee, nipple and closet bend in position, Illus. 59, 69, so closet bend projects distance above tile floor required to sweat or screw to flange. To accurately position closet bend above floor joist, cut a hole for closet bend in a piece of plyscord. Use plyscord same thickness as the sub-flooring previously removed. Place this across joists in position where closet bend is to come through floor. Cut another piece of ¾", or thickness plyscord required. This represents ⅜" tile plus ⅜" exterior grade plywood, Illus. 74. The tile and plywood should equal thickness of finished flooring previously removed. Your tile floor will now be level with adjacent flooring.

You can install line from sewer to tee, or vice versa. In either case, dummy up entire assembly, fittings and pipe, to make certain it comes out right. If in doubt, make a dry run. Hang entire assembly with picture frame wire nailed to joists.

After roughing-in has been completed, nail old sub-flooring to floor joists or nail plyscord of equal thickness. To deaden noise in bathroom, staple a layer of #15 roofing felt over sub-flooring. If you plan on laying ceramic tile, nail ⅜" exterior grade plywood over entire area. Nail every 6" to joists. The ⅜" tile plus ⅜" plywood should equal thickness of original finished flooring.

If you plan on laying vinyl tile, use ⅝" exterior grade plywood instead of ⅜".

Cut shoe off flush with studs at door opening, Illus. 45. If you plan on installing a marble saddle, Illus. 109, place saddle in position, mark outline, cut out finished flooring, install saddle so it finishes at least ¼" higher than tile floor.

## INSTALLATION OF CONVENTIONAL BATHTUB

After ⅜" plywood has been nailed down, bathtub set and connected, 2x4 framing for fixtures nailed in place, apply ⅝" water resistant gypsum backerboard to studs on walls where you want to install ceramic tile; regular ⅝" gypsum board wherever you plan on painting or wallpapering.

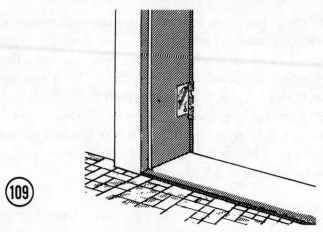

(109)

Lay panel flat, carefully locate and drill holes for stems in diverter valve, tub spout, shower head. Cut holes size needed to allow a socket wrench, Illus. 87, to service stems, Illus. 110, 111. Those who install the fiber glass tub shower, Illus. 6, don't have to go through these steps. This unit comes complete with walls.

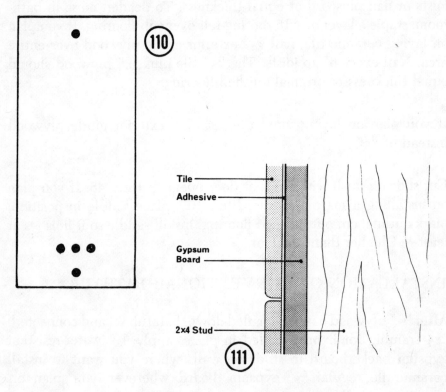

(110)

Tile

Adhesive

Gypsum Board

2x4 Stud

(111)

Do not butt wallboard against edge of tub, Illus.112. Allow ¼″ between water resistant gypsum wallboard and top of tub. Use joint tape and cement to cover joints and corners following wallboard manufacturers' recommendation.

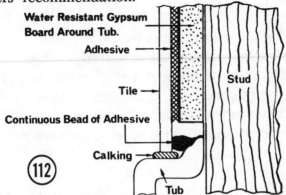

Apply ⅝″ gypsum board to all areas that are to be painted or wallpapered. Use joint tape and cement to cover joints between panels and to cover corners of gypsum board. Follow manufacturer's directions when applying tape and cement. Since escutcheon plates cover stems, small holes aren't important. To lay tile like a "pro," follow step-by-step directions outlined in Easi-Bild Book L06-606, How to Lay Ceramic Tile.

The walls around tub are tiled first. The floor is done after all walls are tiled. After grouting floor tile following directions outlined, allow same to set time grout manufacturer recommends. Cover with heavy building paper and, if convenient, lay a plank or plywood to walk on.

TO INSTALL TOILET

Before fastening floor flange to closet bend, make certain bolt slots in flange allow placing toilet in position desired. Sweat, screw or calk floor flange to closet bend. While some plumbers fasten flange to floor, others prefer not to. This permits flange to ride free if house settles. Those who screw flange to floor, do not fasten it securely. This also allows for movement.

NOTE: If after sweating pipe and fittings in position, the closet bend projects too high, saw it off to height required. If it's too low, cut a nipple to length required and sweat it to bend.

If you have misjudged the height of closet bend, and it's too low to sweat on flange, you can remove tile within area of flange, allow tile to butt against side of flange, then use two wax seals, one on top of the other.

Place bolts in flange in position fixture requires. Lay toilet on side and apply setting compound all around edge, Illus. 113. Place a wax seal, Illus. 113, with or without a vinyl collar, in position on horn of toilet. Some plumbers prefer placing wax seal on flange. Lower toilet straight down while a helper aims bolts through holes in toilet. When bolts are engaged, press toilet in position with just a slight twist.

If you inadvertently mash wax ring, don't try to reshape it. Hold your temper, buy a new wax seal and try again.

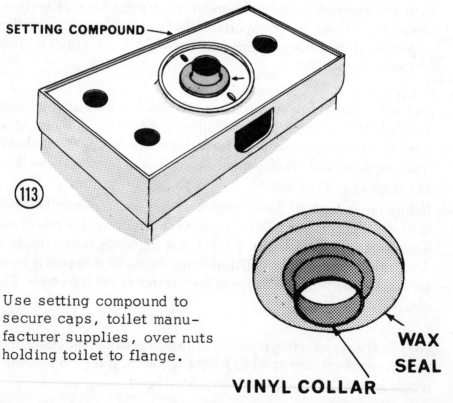

SETTING COMPOUND

(113)

Use setting compound to secure caps, toilet manu-facturer supplies, over nuts holding toilet to flange.

WAX SEAL

VINYL COLLAR

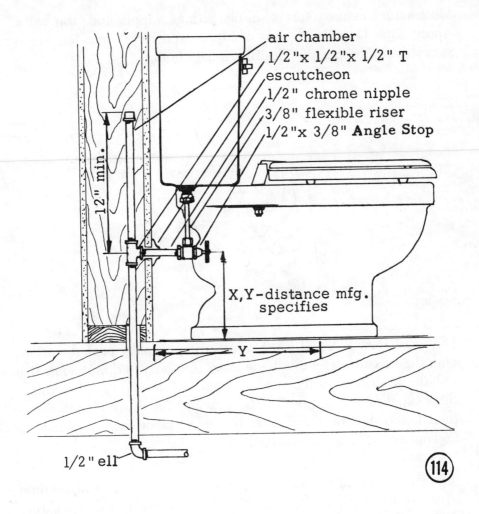

air chamber
1/2"x 1/2"x 1/2" T
escutcheon
1/2" chrome nipple
3/8" flexible riser
1/2"x 3/8" **Angle Stop**

12" min.

X,Y-distance mfg.
specifies

Y

1/2" ell

(114)

If you install a one piece toilet, connect speedy water supply, Illus. 116, to tank. These bend easily so you can compensate for any slight variation.

After bolting toilet in position, clean up setting compound that oozes out from under edge.

Illus. 114 indicates 12" extension for air chamber. This cuts down on air hammers in system. Many retailers sell a fitting that curbs air hammering.

Most fixture manufacturers supply fittings, nipple and stop valve. Apply Tape Dope to threads of nipple and fasten into tee. Screw stop valve to nipple, ⅜" flexible riser to tank.

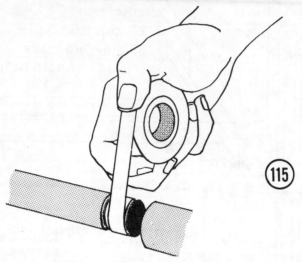

INSTALLING FIXTURES. Manufacturers usually pack directions with their fixture. These provide exact roughing-in dimensions, size of holes to drill, distance lavatory stands off floor on legs manufacturer supplies, etc. If possible, borrow and study installation directions before buying the fixture. In this way you have a chance to find out everything you need to know.

NOTE: As previously mentioned, because of the variance in building materials and their application, plus the continual changes in fixture design, this book should be considered a guide, one that points out various steps. You must always follow manufacturer's directions which frequently allow for a ½" to 1" variation.

The lavatory is fastened to a bracket supplied by manufacturer. The bracket is screwed to backing at height manufacturer recommends.

If water line comes through wall, use an angle stop, Illus. 116. If it comes up through floor, use a straight stop. ⅜" flexible risers are easy to bend.

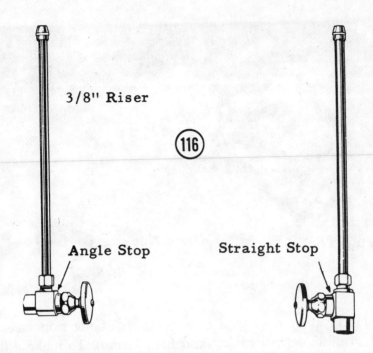

3/8" Riser

Angle Stop        Straight Stop

116

If you want to make more than a small bend in ⅜", ½", even ¾" tubing, use a tube bender, Illus. 87. Just insert tubing in flexible bender and bend to shape required.

To connect an additional lavatory, alongside an existing one, use a three way stop valve, Illus. 117. This has a ½" supply inlet that feeds two ⅜" flexible risers.

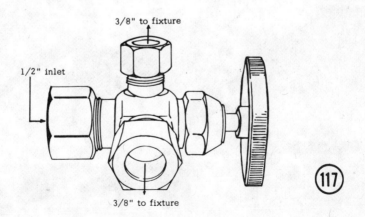

3/8" to fixture

1/2" inlet

117

3/8" to fixture

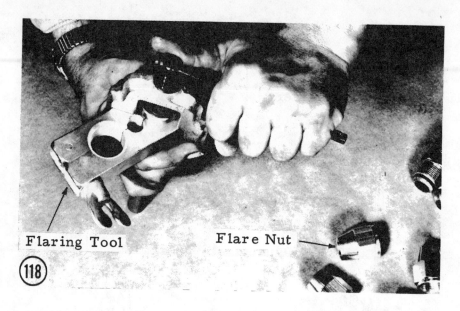

Flaring Tool       Flare Nut

118

To supply a lavatory, or other fixture, at some distance from an existing one, use ⅜" copper tubing and flare fittings. To make a flare
fitting, cut tubing length required. Remove burrs with a knife. Slip
a flare nut A, Illus. 118, over end of tubing. The end of tube is placed
flush with top face of flaring tool. The flaring tool handle is screwed
down to make flare. When end is flared, the nut is fastened to fitting
required. A wide selection of flare fittings are available, Illus. 119.

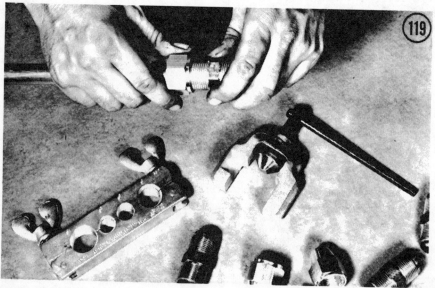

119

## HOW TO ORDER FITTINGS

Wrot solder joint fittings are recommended for all drainage, waste and vent lines. These clean fast, heat up quickly and because of their smooth finish, can't leak when properly sweated.

When ordering always specify size according to Illus. 105.

Refer to the glossary on pages 156 to 158, and charts on pages 132 to 155. Both explain much about the various fittings available. While you may never need more than a handful of different fittings, knowing where each is used helps complete your education as a plumber. Those who plan to extend their interest into a part or full time career will find these charts of great help when studying for a license.

1½", 2" and 3" DWV copper, available in 20 ft. lengths, is recommended for Drainage, Waste and Vent lines.

Always use size codes require.

DWV (drainage, waste and vent) fittings incorporate the recommended drainage pitch (¼" to the foot) for correct gravity flow.

Type L copper is recommended for interior water lines.

If you want to join copper tubing to tubing, you can use a coupling, with a stop, or without a stop, Illus. 99. The stop allows tube to go in only so far, while the coupling without stop permits positioning tube where desired. Couplings are used to join two lengths of copper tube that have the same diameter, couplings are also available that join tubing of different diameters.

## FACTS ABOUT SOLDER.

Solder joints depend on heat, capillary action, melted solder and flux. The flux acts as a lubricant for hot solder, tends to spread solder evenly over surfaces being joined. The capillary action depends on the space between surfaces being soldered.

Solder rated 50-50 tin-lead is considered acceptable for drainage, vent and supply lines. The joints in factory assembled plumbing wall, Illus. 8, are made with 05 5 tin-antimony solder. This is called a silver solder since it is used in the jewelry trade. This makes the strongest joint possible.

50-50 and 95-5 solder is available in a paste type that includes necessary flux. This greatly simplifies soldering, but the following rules must be followed:

Pipe must be cut square. Use a pipe cutter, Illus. 35, or pipe marker and a hacksaw.

All burrs should be filed smooth whether on inside or out. Use a half-round file or pocket knife, Illus. 120.

Both surfaces must be clean of oil, grease, etc.

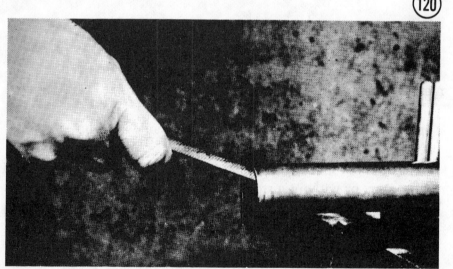

Both surfaces should be sanded, using a fine (00) sand cloth, cleaning pad, or special wire brush available at plumbing supply stores, Illus. 121. Remove all foreign matter, dirt or film. Do not sand off any surface metal. Make certain no particles of dust fly into pipe or fitting. Clean socket of fitting in the same way even though it looks OK.

Apply flux with a small brush, Illus. 122.

If you use Swif, or equal combination of flux and solder, mix thoroughly before using.

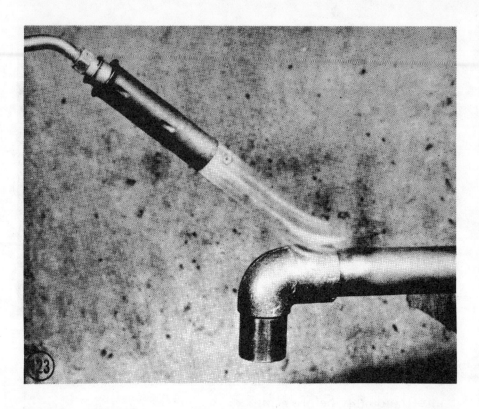

Swif or equal solder requires no separate flux. This permits brushing Swif on both surfaces, joining and twisting parts, then applying heat, Illus. 123. The powdered solder in the 50-50 grade Swif, conforms to SN50 of Federal Spec. QQ-S-571C.

Since a soldered joint depends on capillary action, it requires a fairly tight joint. For this reason, always use proper size fittings and pipe. If there's any question, be sure to center parts to provide equal space all around male end. If you are making up a joint for a horizontal line, and you have any question about the size of joint, position parts and make the solder joint in vertical position, then install in position required.

Always assemble a joint by inserting the pipe into fitting making certain end of tube is against stop in socket. A small twist will help spread flux over both surfaces. Remove excess flux and/or flux/solder with rag.

Apply flame of propane torch on the solder cup of fitting until solder melts, then move flame toward center of fitting until solder is absorbed. Never point flame into a socket. Keep the torch in motion to heat as much area as possible.

When fitting has been heated properly, solder turns from metal grey to black. It will now start to bubble. Remove flame and allow to cool. When bubbling stops, use a damp cloth to brush joint clean.

Avoid overheating. If flux in solder is overheated, it burns away its effectiveness. If this occurs the joint should be opened, cleaned and new solder/flux applied.

IF YOU USE FLUX and SOLDER.
Always bend end of solder wire an amount equal to size of fitting. 1½" bend will usually solder a 1½" fitting, Illus. 124. Heat fitting until solder melts on contact. No additional heat is required. If solder doesn't melt, remove solder, apply heat. Take fitting apart, clean both parts, apply flux and start again.

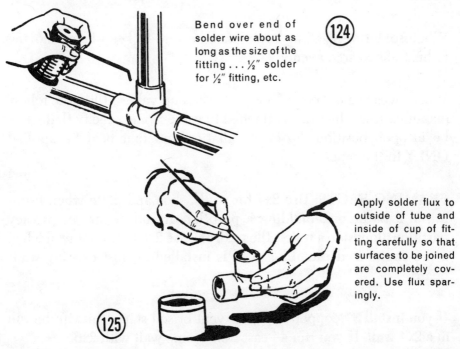

Bend over end of solder wire about as long as the size of the fitting ... ½" solder for ½" fitting, etc.

(124)

Apply solder flux to outside of tube and inside of cup of fitting carefully so that surfaces to be joined are completely covered. Use flux sparingly.

(125)

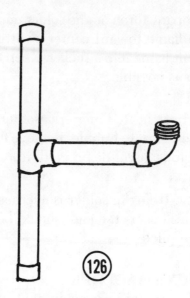

Soldering is an easily acquired skill. Practice on a test assembly, Illus. 126. After soldering and applying a test, remove and clean fittings and try again. You will soon sense when sufficient heat has been applied. If a leak is discovered, remove all water and moisture before starting again.

When soldering 1½" or larger size, be sure to keep flame moving to heat entire area evenly.

When sweating copper tubing to solder cup valves, Illus. 85, follow manufacturer's directions attached to valve. Some specify that valve be in open position during installation and that heat be applied ONLY to the pipe.

FRAMING FACTS. Use 2x4 for studs, shoe and plate when framing in a bathroom, building a partition at end of tub, or privacy partition alongside a toilet, Illus. 20, 45. Use 2x6 to fur out wall when a pre-engineered plumbing wall is installed against existing wallboard.

If you install 3" copper or plastic vent or soil stack, this can be run in a 2x4 wall. If you run 4" cast iron, frame wall with 2x6.

88

A wall or partition is framed with a shoe on floor, plate at top, Illus. 47. Partition at end of a tub is framed in after tub has been installed.

To build a partition at end of tub, Illus. 45, cut shoe and plate to width of tub less ⅝", or thickness of gypsum board used. This will allow gypsum board to finish flush with tub.

If plate on partition runs parallel to ceiling joists, but not under one, nail solid bridging between joists. Nail plate through plaster into joists, Illus. 46.

After plumbing, electrical and heating lines have been roughed-in, all cats and backing nailed in place, insulate an outside wall with rock wool batts. Staple batts to studs following manufacturer's directions.

If you are installing a bathroom over crawl space, rock wool batts should be stapled to floor joists before laying sub-flooring.

FACTS ABOUT PVC AND ABS PIPE AND FITTINGS.

Both provide lifetime service if these simple rules of installation are followed:

1. Cut pipe to length required, using a tube cutter. If same isn't available, use a miter box or make one out of 1x4. Use a cross cut handsaw or hacksaw.

2. Remove burrs and dust, then paint inside of fitting and outside of pipe with No. 1 joint solvent your plastic pipe dealer recommends, using coarse bristle dope brush furnished with each can of solvent.

3. Following directions on can of solvent, paint both surfaces with No. 2 joint solvent.

4. Push pipe into fitting with a twisting motion. At the same time, adjust pipe, or direction of fitting to permit making connection. To be first rate, the connection depends on making it immediately after applying No. 2 solvent.

That's all there is to it. In many installations a complete soil line can be pre-assembled and installed in position. Pipe should be braced every four to six feet. Always brace pipe when making a change in direction, also close to traps. Use metal pipe strap but don't tighten up and distort shape of pipe. Drainage fittings are molded with a ¼" slope per foot pitch.

PVC pipe can be joined to hub of cast iron with oakum and lead. Fittings are available that join PVC to copper.

For those who want to install a bathroom quickly, and with as little labor as possible, the EB Plumbing Wall, Illus. 9, or the Instant Bathroom, Illus. 7, provide two excellent solutions.

INSTALLATION OF PRE-ENGINEERED PLUMBING WALL
No floor flange or closet bend is required when installing the EB Plumbing Wall, Illus. 127. Toilet waste empties into wall inlet, as does drainage from lavatory and bathtub. Since the plumbing wall is easy to install, select any location you desire. It is especially suited to one story houses built on a slab, and in two story installations when you don't want to disturb a ceiling below. Illus. 128 shows some of the many different ways you can install a bathroom with this plumbing unit. It also explains how to order a right or left hand plumbing wall. For left hand installation in a powder room, order #2WHLH; #2WHRH for a right hand.

For a toilet, lavatory and bathtub, left hand installation, order #2-1-WHBO-LH. For a right hand installation, order #2-1-WHBO-RH.

For a bathroom with tub in position shown, order #3WHBO-LH for a left hand; #3WHBO-RH for a right hand.

If you plan on installing an extra bathroom plus a powder room, order #5WHBO-LH for left hand wall installation; #5WHBO-RH for right hand.

The EB Plumbing Wall is 88″ long, 48″ high. The 2x6 framing is 5½″ wide. A wall hung toilet is shipped with this wall, also a 5′0″ bathtub and a 19″ x 17″ lavatory . Illus. 129 shows tub drainage fittings supplied.

A - Connect to 3″ Soil Stack
B - 3″ Vent
C - 3/4″ Water Supply
D - Bathtub Drain
E - 1/2″ supply to Bathtub Diverter Valve
F - Backing for Diverter Valve
G - 1-1/2″ Bathtub Vent
H - Backing for Lavatory Bracket
J - Lavatory Waste
K - Lavatory Supply
L - Backing for Lavatory Supply
M - Toilet Waste
N - Studs Holding Toilet
O - Toilet Supply
P - 1/2″x 3/4″ Reducer
R - Tee - 3″x3″x1-1/2″

Copper tubing and fittings are installed in position at factory.

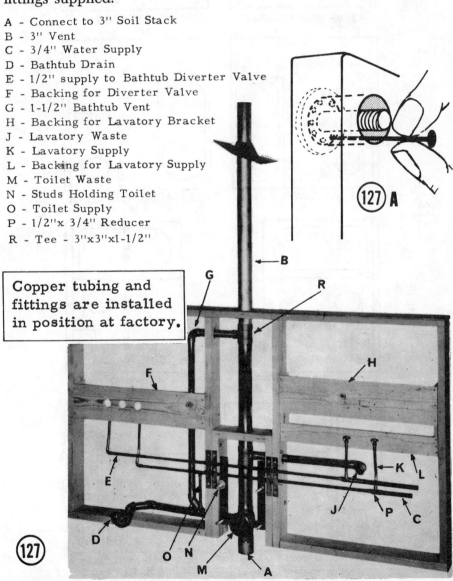

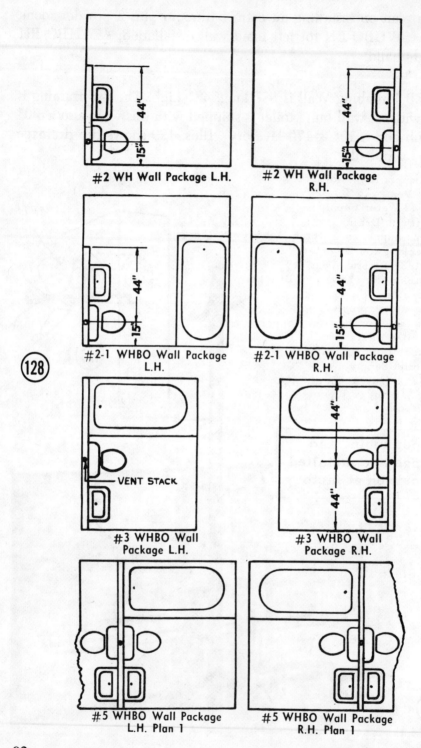

#2 WH Wall Package L.H.

#2 WH Wall Package R.H.

#2-1 WHBO Wall Package L.H.

#2-1 WHBO Wall Package R.H.

VENT STACK

#3 WHBO Wall Package L.H.

#3 WHBO Wall Package R.H.

#5 WHBO Wall Package L.H. Plan 1

#5 WHBO Wall Package R.H. Plan 1

128

When planning for this unit, allow 88″ for recess, Illus. 130, 131. The vent stack is in center, 44″ from either end.

To simplify installation, position unit so vent stack goes between ceiling joists and rafters, and soil stack goes between floor joists. Allow 5′0″ for bathtub.

If you install a kitchen sink or laundry equipment on wall backing up against bathroom, drainage lines permit placing equipment where desired.

The wall hung toilet, supplied with the plumbing wall, fastens to four sturdy bolts fastened to a metal frame. These bolts can be adjusted on the job, or can be set at factory. When ordering the plumbing wall, specify whether wall is to be plastered, then tiled, and specify overall thickness of plaster and tile; or whether you will apply ⅝″ vinyl faced gympsum board and ceramic tile as this book recommends. The factory adjustment costs you nothing and simplifies installation.

The Plumbing Wall can be recessed into a wall, Illus. 9; placed against plaster or plasterboard on existing wall, Illus. 12; or installed as a room divider. No matter how you plan to install it your first consideration is below floor roughing-in, and provision for a 3″ vent.

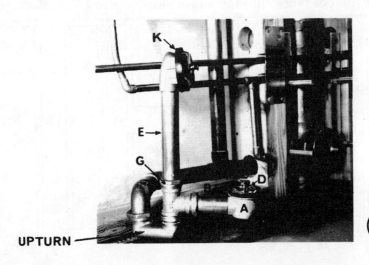

UPTURN

(129)

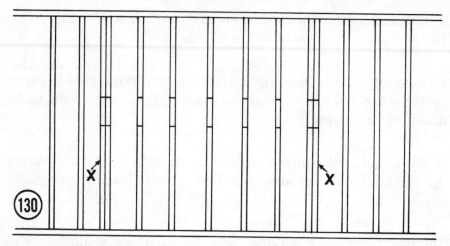

To recess Plumbing Wall, strip plaster off wall that is to receive unit; remove finished flooring within area selected for bathroom. You don't have to take up sub-flooring unless heating equipment requires same.

Place unit in position and draw a line across studs. Nail studs X, Illus. 130 in position indicated. Measure up 9½" or width of 2x10 and mark studs. Make saw cuts 1⅝" deep, or thickness of 2x10. Chisel out notches. Spike a 2x10, cut to length required to studs, using 16 penny common nails, Illus. 131. Cut studs off within area of wall. Cut shoe off flush as indicated. Check plumbing wall with level. Locate holes for soil and vent stack, and supply lines. Remove plumbing wall, cut holes through sub-flooring for soil line, through

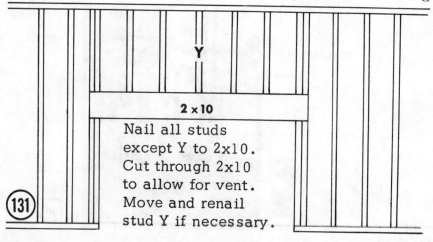

Y

2 x 10

Nail all studs
except Y to 2x10.
Cut through 2x10
to allow for vent.
Move and renail
stud Y if necessary.

ceiling for vent stack, through framing for supply lines. If Plumbing Wall is being installed over a room with a finished ceiling, you can use a 90° elbow to run soil line between floor joists, or drop line below existing ceiling and box it in with an enclosure. To simplify installation, sweat a short length of 3″ copper to A, Illus. 127, prior to placing wall in position. This will simplify connecting soil line when wall is in position.

Replace Plumbing Wall in position, check with level, shim with shingle if necessary, nail frame to studs, floor joists and to 2x10. Connect 3″ vent to existing 3″ or 4″ stack vent, Illus. 31, or saw hole through roof in position 3″ copper vent stack requires. To locate hole, drop a plumb bob down from roof to center of opening for vent, drive a nail through roof to indicate exact position.

After installing a plumbing wall, connect tub drain and overflow as outlined on page 64. Illus. 129 shows fittings provided with EB plumbing Wall.

The bevel rubber washer, K, Illus. 90, is placed between E and outside of tub with thin edge at bottom. These washers usually have raised lines on top and bottom to permit lining up vertically with center of E.

Since inlet D, Illus. 127, receives drainage from bathtub, you don't have to saw a hole through sub-flooring when connecting bathtub to an EB Plumbing Wall.

Backing for bathtub diverter valve and lavatory, nailed in position at factory, permits installing diverter valve and shower according to directions on page 67.

Connect ¾″ supply lines C, Illus. 127, to existing lines at any convenient location. A connection can be made by following directions outlined on page 71.

After setting bathtub and connecting supply and waste lines following procedure previously outlined, cut 2x4's to width required to fur out wall, Illus. 132.

Toenail furring to top of frame and to plate. Nail vinyl covered gypsum board to framing on areas to be tiled, gypsum board on walls to be painted or wallpapered, following directions outlined on page 76. Draw outline of 2x6 framing on wallboard before nailing in position. This will help eliminate driving nails through tubing.

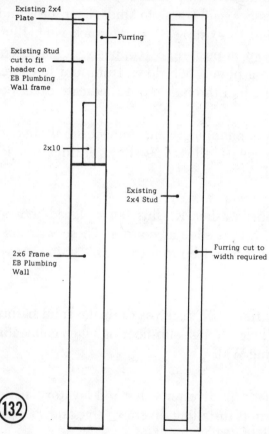

Existing 2x4 Plate

Furring

Existing Stud cut to fit header on EB Plumbing Wall frame

2x10

Existing 2x4 Stud

Furring cut to width required

2x6 Frame EB Plumbing Wall

(132)

When you recess a plumbing wall in 2x4 studs, it requires approximately 2⅞" of floor space; when placed against an existing wall, only 6½". Always remove baseboard and shoe molding before removing finished flooring within area selected. As previously suggested, select a location that allows waste and vent lines to clear floor and ceiling joists and rafter. This eliminates using extra fittings.

If plumbing wall is used as a room divider, soil line can be enclosed in a dummy wall or wall-to-wall closet. Or continue soil line between floor joists to a wall, then across or down a wall to sewer connection.

After setting and connecting bathtub, insulate outside walls. Nail 3/8" exterior grade plywood over sub-flooring. Tile walls and floor following directions previously outlined. Hang wall hung toilet supplied with Plumbing Wall following directions manufacturer supplies.

## TO INSTALL WALL HUNG TOILET

Allowing 1" for gypsum board and ceramic tile, studs for toilet will project approximately 2⅛" from finished wall. 4" waste inlet M, Illus. 127, should protrude 3/8" past finished wall. If 4" inlet does not extend 3/8" beyond finished wall, cut a piece of 4" copper to length required, or purchase an extension nipple from plumbing wall manufacturer. Solder nipple to opening.

> NOTE: The four studs for toilet, and position of waste inlet in plumbing wall must be exact. For this reason, mention exact thickness of gypsum board and tile you plan on using when ordering Plumbing Wall. If necessary, adjustments can be made on the job following manufacturer's directions.

Install 5/8" hex nuts on two lower studs N, and on right upper stud, Illus. 127. Screw the Bowl Saver Nut, Illus. 127A, on the upper left hand stud B. Set all flush with finished wall. Place metal washers supplied on studs.

Place rubber gasket (supplied) in position on outlet of wall hung toilet. Apply a thick ribbon of tub calking along edge of toilet, place toilet in position on studs.

Place fiber washers (supplied) in position and screw chrome cap nuts on two lower and upper right studs.

With 16 penny nail poked through upper left hand hole of toilet, Illus. 127A, turn bowl saver nut counter clockwise until it touches back of bowl. Place fiber washer on this stud, also chrome cap nut. When mounted in this manner, the closet will not bear on finished wall, but will be ⅛" or thickness of washer away. Wipe away excess calking.

Connect tank to toilet with two bolts, following manufacturer's directions. Place large rubber washer A, Illus. 133, in position shown. Place rubber washers B under head of bolt, metal washers C (supplied) under tank. Tighten nuts only as much as is needed. Rubber washer provides the seal. You can easily crack the fixture if force is used.

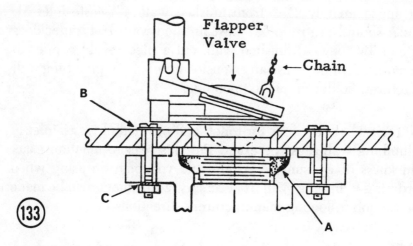

Manufacturer also provides toilet seat. Secure this in position with bolts provided. Connect toilet chain to flapper valve. Allow ⅜" slack in chain following manufacturer's directions.

After walls have been tiled, remove protectors on stems of diverter valve and screw the threaded plastic bushing B, Illus. 134, in position on each stem. The escutcheon plate C, is then screwed on bushing.

The control knob D is pressed into position, cold on right, hot on left, facing fixture. Screws E, provided by control manufacturer, secure knob to stem. Screw tub filler spout G, Illus. 134, on nipple.

Remove galvanized pipe from shower elbow, apply Tape Dope to threads of ½″ chrome shower nipple (supplied), and screw nipple into elbow. Shower head attaches to end of chrome nipple.

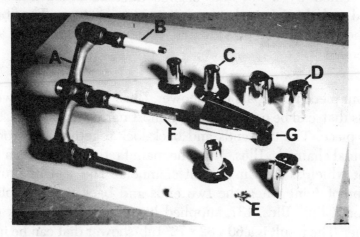

A– Diverter Valve  E– Screw
B– Threaded Bushing  F– Threaded Brass Nipple
C– Escutcheon  G– Tub Spout
D– Control Knob

## LAVATORY INSTALLATION

The Vitreous China Ledge Back Lavatory, supplied with Plumbing Wall, stands 31″ from finished floor. The wall bracket (supplied) is fastened to backing in Plumbing Wall 31″ from floor, or distance manufacturer specifies. Use a carbide tipped bit when drilling through ceramic tile. Use ¼″ x 2″ lag screws to fasten bracket in position. Snug bolts in position but do not tighten or you might crack tile. Hang lavatory on bracket.

Imbed lavatory pop-up drain in gasket compound following procedure outlined on page 64. The 1¼″ tail piece connects to a 1¼″ P Trap that connects to inlet in Plumbing Wall with a compression fitting as described on page 71.

Hot and cold water lines are connected with stop valves and risers provided.

# THE FIBER GLASS BATHTUB

Years ago when codes approved "inside bathrooms," providing they were vented by a fan and flexible duct to an outside wall, it created a whole new market for easy to install fixtures. The fiber glass tub/shower, Illus. 6, provides an economical solution to a costly problem.

The four piece fiber glass tub-shower,[*] Illus. 135, comes in two 60 lb. cartons that can be carried through most narrow doorways. The tub is one piece. The two ends and back lock together in vertical and horizontal channels, Illus. 136. The manufacturer provides a tube of sealant which is used in sealant channels. The sealant provides a waterproof joint when the two ends and back wall are placed in position. Clips, Illus. 137, supplied by manufacturer, lock corners together. The result is a 60 x 32 x 72" tub-shower that can be installed anywhere a drain, supply, vent line and framing permit.

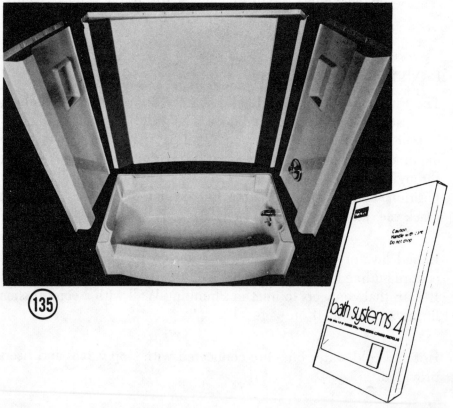

(135)

*Owens-Corning Fiberglas Corporation

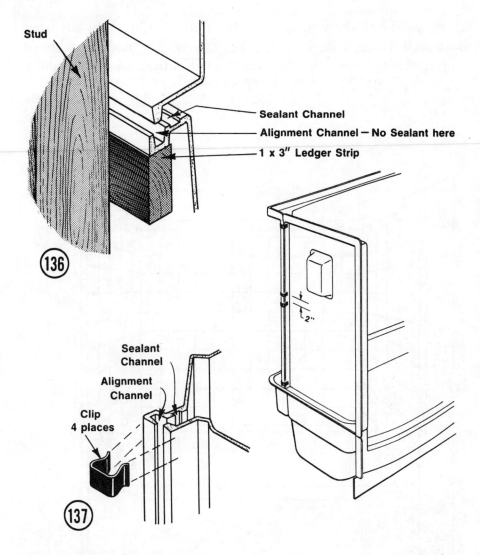

**Stud**

Sealant Channel

Alignment Channel — No Sealant here

1 x 3″ Ledger Strip

(136)

Sealant
Channel

Alignment
Channel

Clip
4 places

2″

(137)

## NEW BATHROOM INSTALLATION

This tub and shower requires framing in exact position noted, Illus. 7. After framing is completed, one man can install the tub and walls in less than an hour. Always read and follow manufacturer's direct‑ ions.

## REMODELING

To remove an existing tub, remove controls, escutcheon, spout, Illus. 94, 89. Cover drain with a rag.

Using a 4' level, draw lines 77" from subfloor, Illus. 138, 30" from back wall. Using a keyhole or saber saw with a blade capable of cutting through ceramic tile, saw through lathe and plaster along drawn lines, BUT DO NOT CUT STUDS.

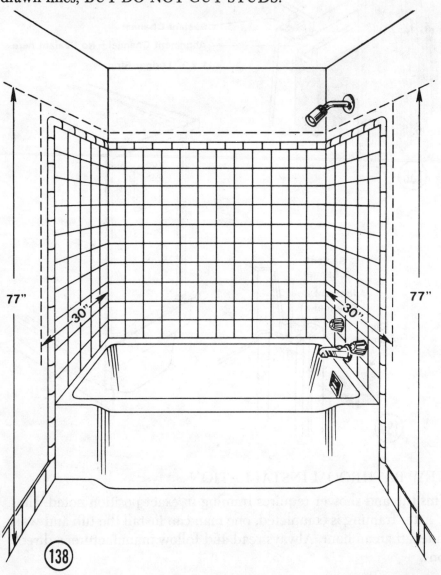

Remove lathe and plaster, tile, and all debris. Disconnect overflow fitting, Illus. 89, 90, and remove drain. This may require Liquid Wrench to loosen. Tap lightly. If drain has cross bars, insert handle of pliers, Illus. 87. Apply leverage with a screwdriver.

Use a wrecking bar to pry back edge of tub up. Tip tub over ceramic tile on floor. Remove tub. Check drain to make certain it's open. If open, plug drain with a rag to keep out debris.

Frame in pocket for tub-shower to exact dimensions shown, Illus 7. Framing should measure 60⅛" across front and back wall. Measure at floor, halfway up and again across at top. Corner of ledger must be square. Shim ledger if necessary to square ends.

(139) LEVEL STRAIGHT EDGED LENGTH OF 2 X 4 OR 2 X 6

Using a 4' level check subfloor in both directions. Nail any loose flooring. If floor slopes, Illus. 139, level with plastic underlayment, Illus. 140. This can be applied feather thin to 5⁄16" thick in one coat. Any number of coats can be applied. When floor is level, measure up 77". Using a level draw lines around enclosure area at 77". Double check height. If floor is uneven and you don't want to use plastic underlayment, place tub in position and check with level, Illus. 141. Use pieces of wood shingle to shim tub level. When level, remove one shim at a time, apply glue and replace shim in place. Allow glue to bond to floor before removing tub.

(140) Latex underlayment can be used to level flooring before nailing plywood. Many tile and carpet adhesives don't bond to latex underlayment.

To simplify installation the center of the tub drain must be 7¾"
from end wall framing, Illus. 142, and 13⅞" from rear wall. Illus.
143. Draw dimensions on floor. Place tub in position. If existing
framing doesn't measure this distance, remove tub and nail 1 x 2 or
strips of plywood, use thickness required, to edge of shoe, studs and
plate. Replace tub. The tub, drain and supply lines must be in position indicated, Illus. 143.

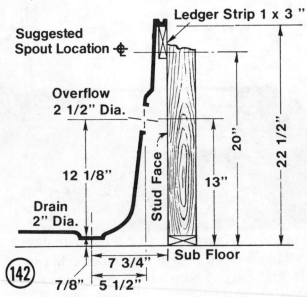

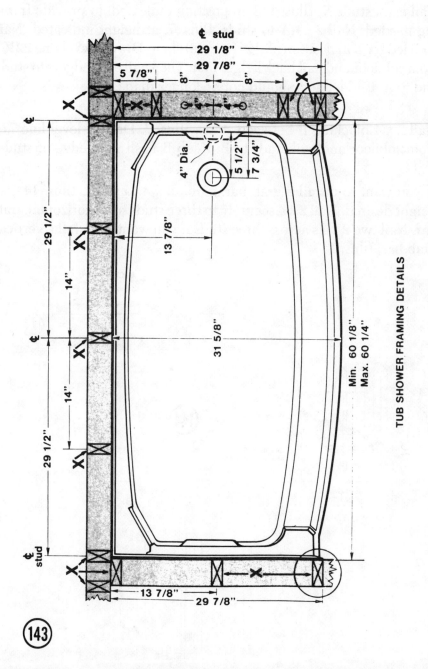

(143)

Tub drain requires a 4″ diameter hole thru floor, 13⅞″ from studs, 2¼″ from a line drawn through center of holes for supply lines.° Holes for supply lines should be 4″ from center as noted, Illus. 143.

° The assembled overflow and drainage pipe, Illus. 149, dictates location of hole through floor.

Nail extra studs X, Illus. 143, in position indicated, to provide framing needed. Nail 2 x 4A to studs, Illus. 7, at height indicated. Nail 1 x 3 ledger B in position, 22½" from subfloor. Draw a level line 22½" from subfloor and nail back ledger first. Then nail end ledgers to studs and to A. End ledgers should not be longer than 28".

Nail 2 x 4 blocking B between studs, Illus. 7. Draw a level line 77" from subfloor and nail studs to B. Keep B flush with edge of studs.

If you want to install a grab bar, nail a 2 x 4 to studs, Illus. 144, at height desired. Nail 2 x 4 securely to three studs for a horizontal grab bar. Nail two 2 x 4's across three studs if you want to install a vertical grab bar, Illus. 145.

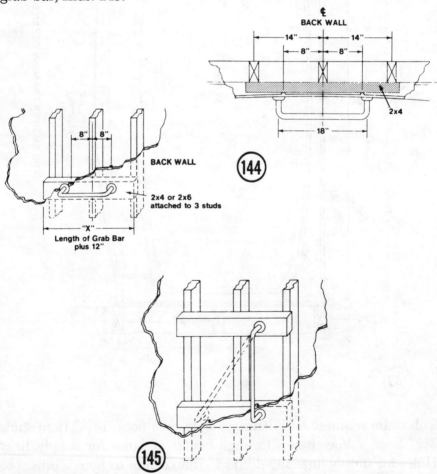

Since you have to drill holes through wall of tub-shower, you can locate grab bar where desired. Reinforcing ribs, molded into the back wall, 8″ on either side of a vertical center line, provide added strength grab bar requires. Grab bar may also be installed on end walls by nailing 2 x 4 in position required. Nail backerboards in position required, Illus. 2.

Rough in supply lines, Illus. 50, using soft copper tubing. Illus. 89 indicates position. Do not strap tubing to backerboard at this stage.

The diverter valve, Illus. 93, 146, is connected to hot and cold supply lines, shower and tub outlet in position shown, Illus. 89.

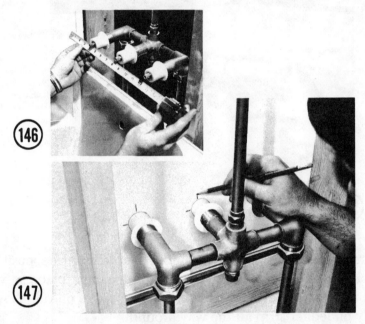

Illus. 147 indicates position of installed shower wall. Finished wall measures 1⅝″ from stud. Allow ⅝″, plus amount needed for escutcheons, when cutting pipe for controls, spout and shower head.

The tub-shower can be assembled within the framing, or outside, then slid into position. To drill holes in exact position shower, spout and controls require, make a template. Rub a little chalk on edge of each pipe and press template against pipe.

Use a 24 x 84" piece of corrugated or hardboard for template. Place it squarely in position against corner framing. Allow ends of pipe to imprint position. Remove and drill ⅛" pilot holes in center. Replace template. If O.K., drill 1" holes through template. Check template again. If O.K., place template in position and drill ⅛" pilot holes in position needed for controls and spout. Apply masking tape to finish on inside of tub and wall. Using a 1" spade bit, or 1" hole saw, drill holes to size controls and spout require, Illus. 148. Drill from inside face. Since manufacturers frequently make design changes, it's necessary to make the installation following directions manufacturer provides.

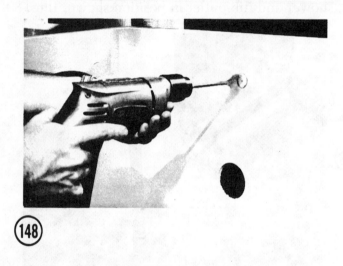

(148)

If studs are exposed and you can assemble the unit in place, position tub and check with level. Leave the tub protector in place so you can stand in tub without marring finish. Note: ledge on tub should rest evenly on ledger strip all the way around.

Assemble overflow tee, Illus. 89, 90, 149. The tub is designed to use a standard 16" adjustable drain and overflow fitting. Apply non-hardening putty or equal sealant to recess in tub, Illus. 142. With gasket B and metal washer C in position shown, Illus. 89, 90, on underside of tub, make up fitting by screwing D into A. Depending on fitting, you can usually turn D with handle or nose of pliers, Illus. 87. Wipe away excess sealant when D is firmly seated.

(149)

Drainage control and overflow pipe E, Illus. 89, 90, fastens to tub with two screws, and to F with a slip joint compression nut and washer G in position shown. The thinnest part of beveled rubber washer K is normally placed down. Since manufacturers frequently make design changes, always follow directions manufacturer provides. Screw nipple H into F using a strap wrench, Illus. 87. You can also wrap adhesive tape around H and tighten with a pair of pliers or a stillson wrench, or fasten a pipe clamp to H. Use pliers on clamp.

The tub-shower has both alignment and sealant channels, Illus. 137. Follow manufacturer's directions and apply sealant manufacturer provides, Illus. 150, in sealant channels. Do not put sealant in an alignment channel. Keep this clean.

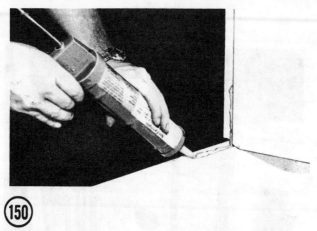

(150)

If framing on back and end walls is accessible, apply a continuous ⅛" bead of sealant in horizontal sealant channel. Place back wall in position and seat wall securely in alignment channel.

Apply a ⅛" bead of sealant to vertical sealant channel farthest from plumbing wall. Apply sealant to horizontal sealant channel on this end. Position this end wall and seat securely in both horizontal and vertical joints. Do the same for end wall on plumbing end.

Fasten corners with clips provided, Illus. 137. Use 4 clips in position indicated, 2 clips 2" apart at center, one clip at top and bottom. Using a wet cloth wipe away excess sealant.

PULL DOWN

(151)

Exerting downward pressure, Illus. 151, nail wall with big head #6 galvanized roofing nails through holes at corners. If you question your nailing skill, use a piece of aluminum or hardboard to protect finish while nailing. Illus. 152.

Nail end panels in position. Start nailing at back wall. Make certain nails keep all joints tight. If nailing pulls a joint open, use shims. Drive nails into mid points of end panels. Nail back wall flange starting at center. Fasten vertical nailing flange at front. Wipe away excess sealant with a wet cloth. Fasten the tub apron nailing flange to studs starting at top and working down.

If back corners of recess are not accessible, do this. Install tub as previously described. Apply sealant where required and assemble end walls to back wall. Apply sealant to channel on tub. Position assembled wall sections on tub. Nail flanges as previously described.

Calk all openings around valve and spout with water resistant sealer, Illus. 153. Your tub-shower dealer sells a mildew resistant sealer that may be used to seal external seams. Because this material forms a skin fast, then becomes difficult to smooth, make a practice run before applying. Only apply an 8 or 10″ length bead at a time. Wipe smooth with your finger, Illus. 154. Remove excess. If you apply masking tape to both sides of each joint, you can do a better job.

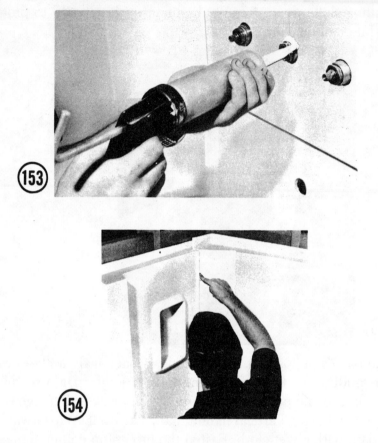

To finish installation from top of wall enclosure to ceiling, nail ⅛″ furring strips to studs, Illus. 155. Apply water resistant sealer to top edge of wall. Apply ½″ gypsum board with factory finished paper bound edge down towards tub enclosure. Leave a ¼″ sealant joint between edge of wallboard and enclosure. Nail wallboard to studs. Drive first course 1¼″ above enclosure wall. Follow tub-shower manufacturer's directions to clean up unit. Apply controls, spout, shower head. Fasten supply lines to backerboard with pipe clamps or strap.

The tub opening is 57¾″. Shower enclosures may be installed with self tapping screws, molly fasteners or toggle bolts.

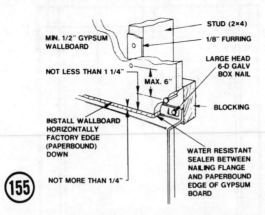

Figure labeled 155, with the following callouts:

MIN. 1/2" GYPSUM WALLBOARD

STUD (2×4)

1/8" FURRING

NOT LESS THAN 1 1/4"

LARGE HEAD 6-D GALV BOX NAIL

MAX. 6"

BLOCKING

INSTALL WALLBOARD HORIZONTALLY FACTORY EDGE (PAPERBOUND) DOWN

NOT MORE THAN 1/4"

WATER RESISTANT SEALER BETWEEN NAILING FLANGE AND PAPERBOUND EDGE OF GYPSUM BOARD

To service a tub trap and diverter valve, install an inspection panel in wall backing up plumbing, Illus. 53. Dash lines indicate position of a removable plywood or hardboard panel. Screw or hinge panel in position. Cut panel full width of two studs by 26" high.

## HOW TO INSTALL A SHOWER STALL

While manufacturers of pre-fabricated molded plastic, metal and stone shower stalls provide step-by-step directions which must be followed, this is the general procedure.

Select size. Stalls are available in sizes ranging from 32x32, 36x36, 42x34, up to 60x32. To simplify installation, let's assume you are installing a 32" x 32", Illus. 156. Build 2x4 framing following directions on page 41. Allow 32" x 32" inside dimensions.

The shower floor should be placed on level sub-flooring. Locate center and check floor in two directions using a 2 ft. level. Cut a 4¾" hole (or size specified) in center, 16" from each wall.

Most pre-fab shower stalls come with 2" drain that connects to 2" pipe and P Trap. Rough-in 2" pipe, ¼" above sub-flooring, or height drain fixture requires; also run ½" supply lines following directions outlined.

Place shower floor in position. Calk drain housing to drain pipe using oakum calking and hot lead, or method recommended, Illus. 157.

113

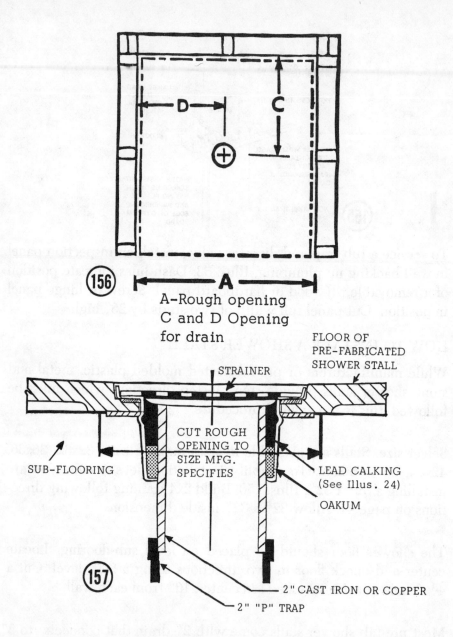

A–Rough opening
C and D Opening
for drain

STRAINER

FLOOR OF
PRE-FABRICATED
SHOWER STALL

CUT ROUGH
OPENING TO
SIZE MFG.
SPECIFIES

SUB-FLOORING

LEAD CALKING
(See Illus. 24)

OAKUM

2" CAST IRON OR COPPER

2" "P" TRAP

Nail ⅝" gypsum board as described on page 76 to inside of shower stall. Space factory sealed edge distance from edge of stall manufacturer specifies. Nail sides to studs as previously described. Seal joint with sealant specified, Illus. 158. Use care not to break or cut factory sealed edge. Apply ceramic tile on walls of bathroom as explained in Book L06-606.

114

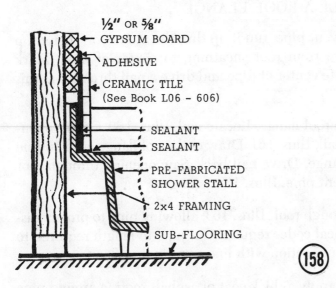

½" OR ⅝"
GYPSUM BOARD
ADHESIVE
CERAMIC TILE
(See Book L06 - 606)
SEALANT
SEALANT
PRE-FABRICATED
SHOWER STALL
2x4 FRAMING
SUB-FLOORING

(158)

SEALANT NOTE: Don't butt gypsum board against edge of stall. Allow clearance for bead of sealant. Follow manufacturer's directions.

Shower stalls equipped with glass or plastic walls provide a filler channel that fasten to shoulder of floor pan. A metal frame is then fastened in position shown, Illus. 159, with sheet metal self-tapping screws.

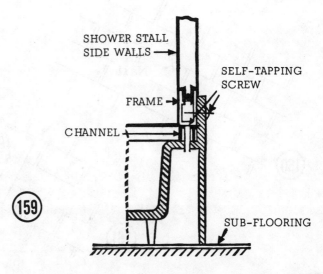

SHOWER STALL
SIDE WALLS
SELF-TAPPING
SCREW
FRAME
CHANNEL
(159)
SUB-FLOORING

# HOW TO INSTALL A ROOF FLANGE

When installing a vent pipe, run it up thru the attic floor, then drop a plumb bob down from roof sheathing to center of pipe. Mark sheathing to indicate center of pipe and drive a nail thru roof at this point.

Go up on roof with roof flange. Locate nail, Illus. 160. Center opening in flange over nail, Illus. 161. Draw outline of flange, also outline of hole. Remove flange. Drive nail back. Saw opening through roof to accommodate vent pipe, Illus. 162

Place vent pipe through roof, Illus. 163, allowing pipe to project distance above roof local codes require. Cut pipe to length required to make a one piece connection with line coming thru floor.

Raise shingles and apply a thick coat of asphalt roofing around pipe and on area to be covered by flange, Illus. 164.

Slip flange over pipe and under raised shingles. Cut shingles to shape shown. Nail flange in position, Illus. 165. Relay shingles in a bed of asphalt roofing. Face nail shingles where required. Paint nail heads with asphalt. Using a hammer, bend flange tight around vent pipe. Carefully seal joint with a neat line of asphalt paste roofing.

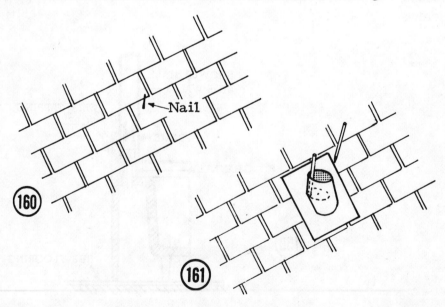

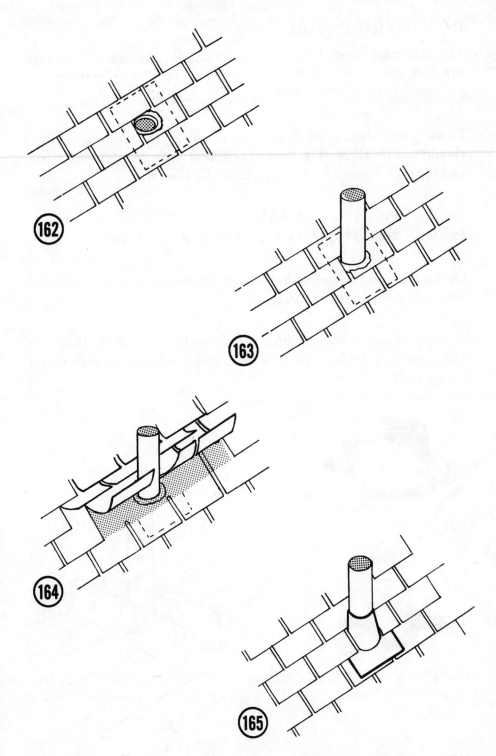

## HOW TO BRACE A SOIL STACK

The soil stack must be braced as it is being installed. Use pipe brackets, straps and/or floor flange, Illus. 166. Your plumbing supply retailer stocks brackets designed for each kind of pipe.

Bracing an existing soil stack before cutting is very important. It should not be allowed to shift or sag. Bolt pipe strap around barrel and/or under a hub, nail straps to studs, Illus. 4.

Another good way is to clamp barrel or hub between two 2x4's. Use ½" x 10" bolts. Place 2x4's across floor joists, Illus. 167.

Or support hub between 2x4 braces toenailed to floor. Nail cross braces in position shown, Illus. 168.

Or support hub or barrel with a 1x4 nailed between studs, Illus. 169. Slip pipe strap under hub. Nail strap to top edge of support with 6 penny nails.

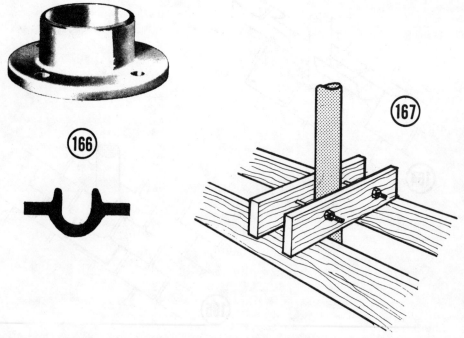

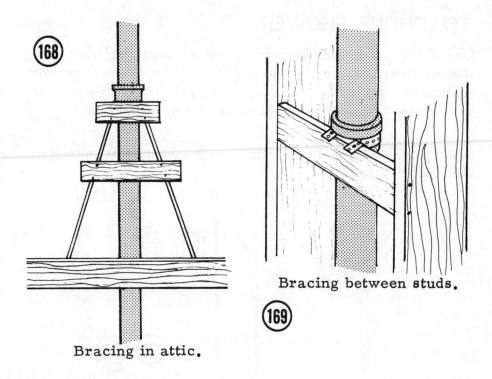

Bracing between studs.

Bracing in attic.

For Additional Information

The tools, materials, pipe, fittings and products, the EB Plumbing Wall and Instant Bathroom described in this book are currently available. Your Easi-Bild retailer can order a plumbing wall for right hand or left hand installation and can quote a price for this unit, delivered to your home.

Place orders for all fittings, products, plumbing wall and/or pre-fabricated bathroom with your retailer. When ordering the Plumbing Wall, specify whether framing is to be covered with ½" or ⅝" gypsum board and tile; or plaster and tile; or just wallboard. Specify total thickness. Also indicate arrangement you want as shown on page 92. Always order fittings by name used in book.

The author does not endorse or recommend any specific product or the manufacturer's method of installation, but does endeavor to show those products, tools and materials that simplify solving a particular problem.

# TELEPHONE SHOWER

One of the latest devices designed for better living is the "telephone" shower, Illus. 170. This easy to install, hand held shower permits washing any part without wetting others. It is particularly popular with women who want to shower without wetting their hair.

Those who don't have a bidet find this device almost as efficient in cleansing vital areas.

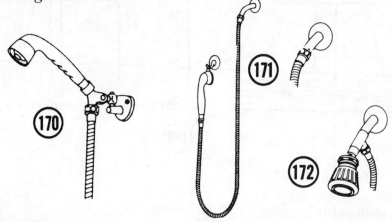

The telephone shower consists of a flexible hose that can be fastened directly to existing shower arm, Illus. 171. Or you can keep your shower and use the diverter connection, Illus. 172.

If you prefer to do away with showerhead and make a closefitting connection, a replacement elbow, Illus. 173, is also available. If your bath doesn't have a shower, remove discharge nozzle and replace with adapter spout, Illus. 174.

Be sure to insert washer between new fitting and threaded stud.

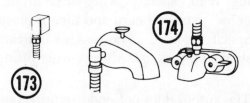

If you don't have an adjustable end wrench that fits your shower connection, wrap the connection with masking tape and use a pair of ARC joint pliers, Illus. 87.

# FIXTURE DETAILS

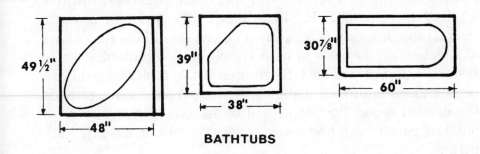

**BATHTUBS**

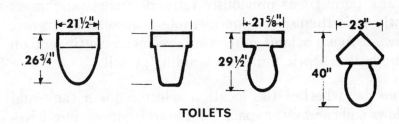

**TOILETS**

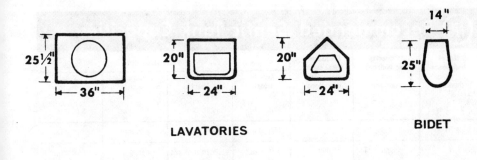

**LAVATORIES**

**BIDET**

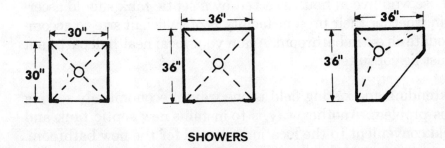

**SHOWERS**

# FACTS ABOUT A SEPTIC TANK

Before buying property in an undeveloped area, inquire whether the Board of Health will issue a permit for a septic tank. If the property is adjacent to a stream or lake that's part of a watershed, or close to wells supplying a community water system, a permit will only be granted if the tank and field can be placed an approved distance. If the parcel doesn't provide the needed space, no permit will be issued. In many areas, a building permit won't be issued unless you obtain a septic tank permit.

Before signing any purchase agreement, ascertain whether a septic tank permit was previously refused. Smart purchasers frequently save themselves considerable heartache by having their lawyer make a land purchase agreement contingent on obtaining both a septic tank and building permit.

Also consider whether the location selected for a tank and field allows sufficient clear space for a house, garage and driveway. Illus. 175, indicates the various size tanks required for 2, 3, 4 and 5 bedroom houses.

## (175) Recommended Septic Tank Capacities

| No. of bedrooms in dwelling | Capacity per bedroom in gallons | Required total tank capacity in gallons | Tank size | | | |
|---|---|---|---|---|---|---|
| | | | Inside width | Inside length | Liquid depth | Total depth |
| 2 or less | 375 | 750 | 3 ft. 6 in. | 7 ft. 6 in. | 4 ft. 0 in. | 5 ft. 0 in. |
| 3 | 300 | 900 | 3 ft. 6 in. | 8 ft. 0 in. | 4 ft. 6 in. | 5 ft. 6 in. |
| 4 | 250 | 1,000 | 4 ft. 0 in. | 8 ft. 0 in. | 4 ft. 6 in. | 5 ft. 6 in. |
| 5 | 250 | 1,250 | 4 ft. 0 in. | 9 ft. 0 in. | 4 ft. 6 in. | 5 ft. 6 in. |

Those who live in houses served by a septic tank should ascertain whether their present facility is of sufficient size to accommodate an extra bathroom. Again your local health department must be consulted.

Extending an existing field is one way of economically solving this problem. Another way is to install a new septic tank and field convenient to the location selected for the new bathroom.

Prospective property buyers who plan on building outside of a sewer district, should study the installation of a septic tank and field, as it's important in making the property usable. Most rural communities adjacent to any size city, only permit installation if it's placed 5' or more from the house, at least 50' from a cistern, 100' from a well, and that the field is not closer than 10' from property line, Illus. 176.

When selecting a site be sure to consider wells, cisterns, or streams on your neighbor's property.

As noted in Illus. 176, 177, codes specify hub and spigot, or hubless cast iron sewer pipe between house and septic tank. This must be 5'0" or longer. Cast iron or bituminous sewer pipe is acceptable between the septic tank and either a junction or distribution box.

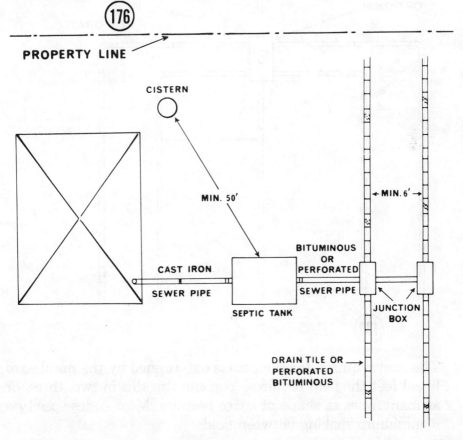

(176)

PROPERTY LINE

CISTERN

MIN. 50'

MIN. 6'

CAST IRON SEWER PIPE

SEPTIC TANK

BITUMINOUS OR PERFORATED SEWER PIPE

JUNCTION BOX

DRAIN TILE OR PERFORATED BITUMINOUS

The sewer line between house and septic tank must slope at least ¼″ to 1″ per foot, as does the connection between the tank and the junction box. Follow local code requirements. The septic tank must be level.

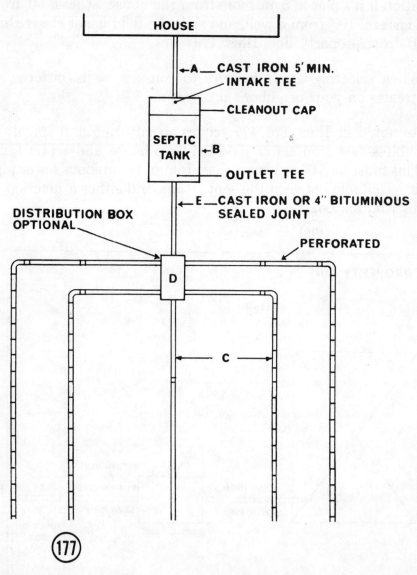

HOUSE

A — CAST IRON 5′ MIN.
INTAKE TEE

CLEANOUT CAP

SEPTIC TANK ←B

OUTLET TEE

E — CAST IRON OR 4″ BITUMINOUS
SEALED JOINT

DISTRIBUTION BOX OPTIONAL

PERFORATED

D

C

(177)

The area required for the field is determined by the number of lineal feet the field requires. You can run this in two, three, or as many rows as shape of space permits. Most codes specify a 6′ minimum spacing between fields.

A septic tank and field should never be located in a low, wet area, or on rock, and only in an open area where no tree roots, shrubbery, etc., will send roots down to the tile. After selecting a site, call the Department of Health and they will make a free inspection or will advise what must be done to pass inspection.

Most inspectors not only inspect the site, make inquiry concerning the number of bedrooms the house will contain, recommend size of tank, shape, and length of field, but will also make an absorption test to ascertain how fast the subsoil will absorb water. Or they will advise you how to make a test.

While installing a system is relatively simple, a septic tank installation can become real sticky when you learn that such and such a septic tank company can obtain a permit for you, then quotes an exorbitant cost.

Regardless of what an "in" septic tank company may tell you, no one can stop you from making your own installation, providing you follow local regulations.

If you think anyone in the health department is giving you a hard time, there are two good reasons why this may be so. Most health departments make an honest and determined effort to protect the area adjacent to water shed property. Regardless of whether it's a nearby stream, runoff into a stream, or a well on your property, or neighboring property, the field must be laid according to regulations. The second reason is financial. If a local septic company has a monopoly, they may overcharge.

If you read and learn how to install a septic tank before you start talking business to an installer, you will save yourself a lot of time, money and aggravation. If you then decide to do part or all the work, you can save even more money. Either way, you get a better job when you know what needs to be done.

A septic tank system consists of a large metal or concrete holding tank B, Illus. 177; a distribution center D; and a field of 4" diameter perforated drain tile, C. Many codes permit installation without a distribution box. They allow junction boxes as shown in Illus. 176.

The sewer line E, Illus. 177, must be 4″ hub and spigot or hubless cast iron, 5′0″ or more in length. Hubless 4″ cast iron, now available in many areas, is also approved by most health departments.

You can buy a metal septic tank or a prefabricated concrete one, or build a 6″ form, and pour the concrete tank in place. Reinforce sides and bottom with ½″ rods, or use 6x6 reinforcing wire.

Since tanks purchased readymade will be delivered by a truck with a crane that positions the tank level in the excavation you have prepared, the question you must resolve is whether the site selected for the tank can be reached by a truck. Give consideration to this simple but important fact since once you start excavating for a house you might not be able to truck and crane a tank into position.

If you prefer to pour a tank in place, will a ready mix truck be able to come close enough to chute or wheelbarrow the ready mix? Or does the location of the site automatically require you to rent a concrete mixing machine and do the work on the site? With planks properly placed to form a level, or downhill walk, two or three willing souls can usually wheelbarrow concrete from a ready mix truck fast enough to pour a tank without paying overtime for a waiting truck. If you decide to buy ready mix, ask the company how long you can hold the truck on the job before overtime sets in.

Always check tank with a level after it's placed in position, and before the truck leaves.

Trenches for a field are usually 18″ wide and to a depth that permits 4″ to 6″ of gravel on bottom, 4″ tile, plus 2″ to 4″ of gravel on top, Illus. 178. The 4″ drain tile used in the field must be placed at a pitch codes specify. This could be 2″ to 4″ in 100′.

126

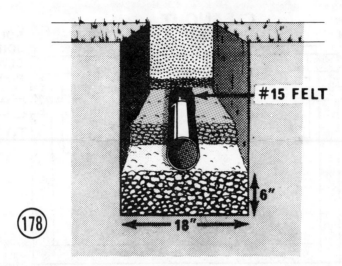

#15 FELT

6″

18″

(178)

Building a form and pouring a tank is only recommended when you have alienated the affection of local suppliers.

If you buy a prefab, buy the size your house requires, or one size larger. Buy a size that would be required if you add extra bedrooms at some date in the future. There is no economy in putting in a minimum approved size when a larger size only costs a few dollars more.

If you buy a complete installation, the installer will dig the hole for the tank and trench the field. If you decide to dig it, be sure to excavate to exact depth the Health Department suggests, and make certain bottom is level. Use a straight 2x4 and a level to check bottom of excavation. The depth and size of hole for a tank is determined by its size and shape.

Since the sewer line from the house to the tank must pitch ¼″ per foot, or pitch local codes require, the depth of the hole will be determined by the intake TEE, Illus. 179. Dig trench from house to selected site. Slope trench to pitch pipe requires. When 5′0″ or further away, place a TEE, Illus. 180, in position on the end of the pipe. To estimate depth of excavation, measure from bottom of TEE to depth below TEE your tank requires. Note position of inlet TEE, Illus. 179.

Codes recommend outlet TEE be placed 3″ lower than inlet.

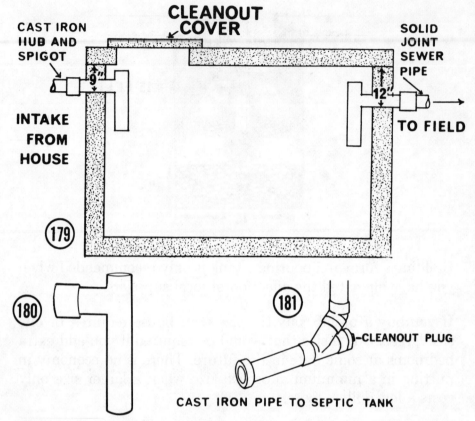

CLEANOUT COVER

CAST IRON HUB AND SPIGOT

INTAKE FROM HOUSE

SOLID JOINT SEWER PIPE

TO FIELD

9"

12"

179

180

181

CLEANOUT PLUG

CAST IRON PIPE TO SEPTIC TANK

When installing a new tank, always install a cleanout plug, Illus. 181, in direct line with the inlet TEE. This greatly simplifies servicing a septic tank.

When installing a septic tank on rolling or hilly land the field should follow the contour of the land.

A septic tank can also be built with concrete blocks. Excavate to size and depth tank requires. Level bottom, then dig a 10" wide footing trench, 4" lower than floor, around perimeter of floor area. Lay a thick bed of mortar and position a starter course of 10x8x16 or 18" blocks. These will project 4" above the floor area.

Cut 6x6 reinforcing wire to size floor area requires. Raise wire about 1" and pour floor flush with top of block. Fill cores of blocks with concrete. Allow slab to set three days, then build walls using 8x8x16 or 18″ blocks. These are placed flush with inside edge of 10″ block. Fill cores of the first three courses of blocks with concrete. If you are building a large tank, lay reinforcing wire, in every third course of block.

Set Inlet Tee and Outlet Tee in position shown, Illus. 179.

Allow tank to set at least five days, then paint inside and outside with hot tar or asphalt cement.

Follow local code requirements, and lay field to depth specified. Cover with size and depth of gravel specified, then cover gravel with #15 felt before backfilling. Since the Board of Health will want to make an inspection before you cover the field, follow directions they provide, and under no circumstances give the inspector a hard time.

Cover tank with precast slabs, **Illus. 182.**

When laying perforated bituminous field tile, follow local code recommendations regarding a distribution box, Illus. 177, or junction boxes, Illus. 176.

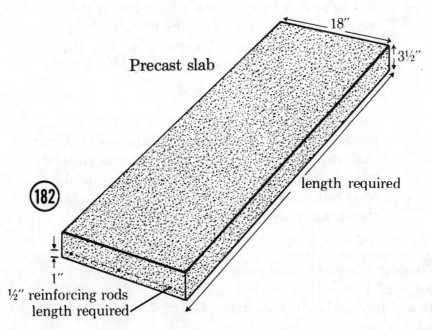

Precast slab

18″

3½″

length required

(182)

1″

½″ reinforcing rods
length required

# HOW TO THINK METRIC

Government officials concerned with the adoption of the metric system are quick to warn anyone from attempting to make precise conversions. One quickly accepts this advice when they begin to convert yards to meters or vice versa. Place a metric ruler alongside a foot ruler and you get the message fast.

Since a meter equals 1.09361 yards, or 39⅜″+, the decimals can drive you up a creek. The government men suggest accepting a rough, rather than an exact equivalent. They recommend considering a meter in the same way you presently use a yard. A kilometer as 0.6 of a mile. A kilogram or kilo as just over two pounds. A liter, a quart, with a small extra swig.

To more fully appreciate why a rough conversion is preferable, note the 6″ rule alongside the metric rule. A meter contains 100 centimeters. A centimeter contains 10 millimeters.

As an introduction to the metric system, we used a metric rule to measure standard U.S. building materials. Since a 1x2 measures anywhere from ¾ to ²⁵⁄₃₂ x 1½″, which is typical of U.S. lumber sizes, the metric equivalents shown are only approximate.

Consider 1″ equal to 2.54 centimeters;
10″ = 25.4 cm.
To multiply 4¼″ into centimeters: 4.25 × 2.54 = 10.795 or 10.8 cm.

# APPENDIX

## COPPER - CAST IRON FITTINGS
## PLASTIC

### FIXTURE UNIT VALUES

| FIXTURE | UNIT VALUE | TRAP AND DRAIN PIPE SIZE |
|---|---|---|
| 1 bathroom group consisting of water closet, Lavatory, and bathtub or shower stall. | 6-8 | |
| Bathtub (with or without shower) | 2 | 1½" |
| Bidet | 3 | Nominal—1½" |
| Kitchen sink (Domestic) | 2 | 1½" |
| Kitchen sink (Domestic with food disposer) | 3 | 1½" |
| Lavatory | 1 | Small PO 1¼" |
| Lavatory | 2 | Large PO 1½" |
| Shower Stall (Domestic) | 2 | 2" |
| Water Closet: | | |
| Tank Operated | 4 | 3" |

1

2

D W V

3

4

D W V

13

5

6

DWV

7

D W V

8

9

10

11

1½
1½
1½
1½

12

13

A
C
B

Drawing for 3"

C
B
A

Drawing for 4"

# COPPER FITTINGS

**1** Sanitary Tee. Copper to Copper to Copper.
Available in many different sizes. To indicate size specify number 1, 2 and 3 in order indicated.

**2** Fitting Sanitary Tee. Fitting to Copper to Copper.

**3** Soil Pipe Adapter. Connects Soil Pipe Hub to Copper tube.
Available in many different sizes.

**4** Quarter Bend 90°. Copper to Fitting.
Also used as a closet bend with floor flange No. 13.

**5** 90° Sanitary Tee with Slip-Joint.
Joins copper tube to chrome or brass drain from lavatory or bathtub.

**6** Quarter Bend 90°. Copper to Copper long turn.
Joins two lengths of copper tube.

**7** Quarter Bend 90°. Copper to Copper.

**8** Sanitary Tee with Side Inlet on Left.
Copper to Copper to Copper to Copper.

**9** Sanitary Tee with Side Inlet on Left and Right.

**10** Stack Fitting with Left Inlet.
Provides inlet for toilet, also 1½" or 2" inlet for drainage line.

**11** Stack Fitting with Right and Left Inlet.

**12** Double Sanitary Tee. Copper to Copper to Copper to Copper.
Used where code requires separate vents to main stack.
Available 3" x 3" x 1½" x 1½" and many other sizes.

**13** Closet Flange attaches toilet to closet bend. Quarter Bend 90°, Illus. 4, can be used as a closet bend.

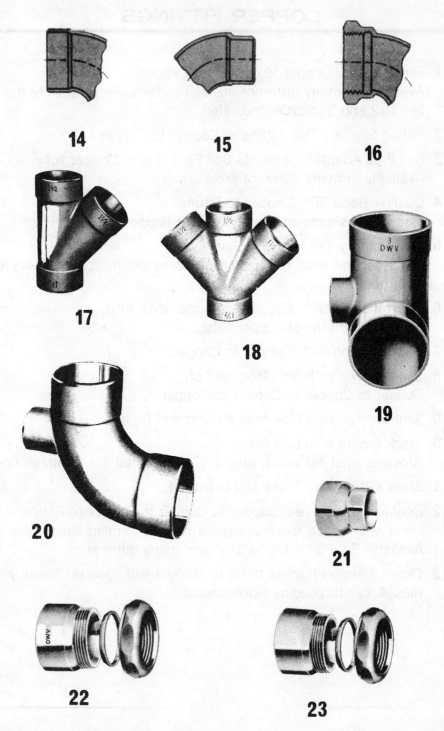

**14**

**15**

**16**

**17**

**18**

**19**

**20**

**21**

**22**

**23**

# COPPER FITTINGS

**14** Solder Cup End.

**15** Fitting End. This end goes into fitting.

**16** Usually designated FPT or FSPS. Female pipe thread or female standard pipe size.

**17** 45° Y-Branch. Copper to copper to copper.
Joins main line with copper branch line.

**18** 45° Double Y-Branch.

**19** Quarter Bend (90°) with side inlet. Copper to Fitting to Copper. Fitting End sweats to closet flange. Side inlet simplifies connecting drainage line from lavatory and/or bathtub.

**20** Quarter Bend (90°) with High Heel Inlet.
Copper to copper to copper.

**21** Fitting Reducer. Fitting to copper.

**22** Coupling with Slip-Joint Connection.
Joins copper tube to chrome or brass waste line from lavatory or bathtub.

**23** Fitting Slip-Joint Adapter.
Joins fitting to chrome or brass waste line from lavatory or bathtub.

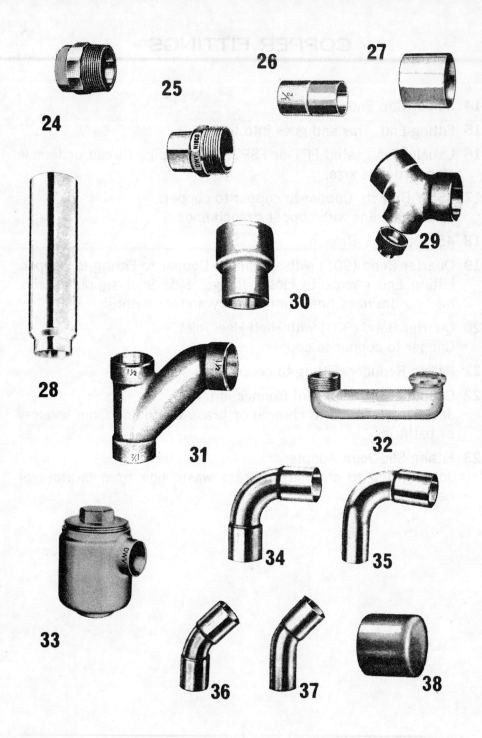

# COPPER FITTINGS

**24** Male Adapter — Copper to MSPS.
Joins copper tube to threaded female.

**25** Male Fitting Adapter — Fitting to MSPS.
Joins fitting to threaded female.

**26** Coupling with stop. Copper to copper.

**27** Repair coupling. No stop.

**28** Roof Vent Increaser — Copper to Fitting.
3" x 4" x 18" or 24" or 30" long.

**29** Eighth Bend (45°) with cleanout, used in line where cleanout is required.

**30** Vent Increaser — Copper to Copper.
Can be used to change diameter of vent stack just before going through roof. Available in wide combination of sizes — 1½" x 4", 1½" x 3", etc.

**31** Long Turn T-Y. Also available with side inlet on branch.

**32** Upturn MSPS fastens to bottom of one piece drum trap #33.
Bathtub outlet connects to Slip Joint.

**33** Drum Trap — One piece. Inlet from bathtub in bottom, outlet in top.

**34** 90° Elbow — Copper to Copper.
Available in short or long radius.

**35** 90° Ell Short Radius, also available long radius.
Copper to Fitting.

**36** 45° Elbow — Copper to Copper.

**37** 45° Fitting to copper ell.

**38** Cap.

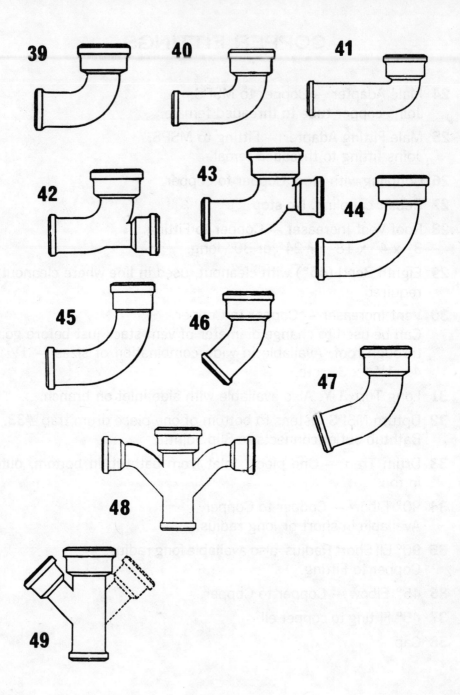

**39**  **40**  **41**

**42**  **43**  **44**

**45**  **46**  **47**

**48**

**49**

# CAST IRON

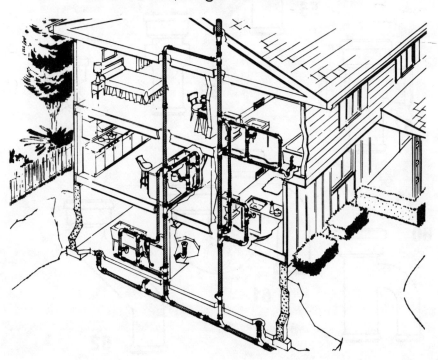

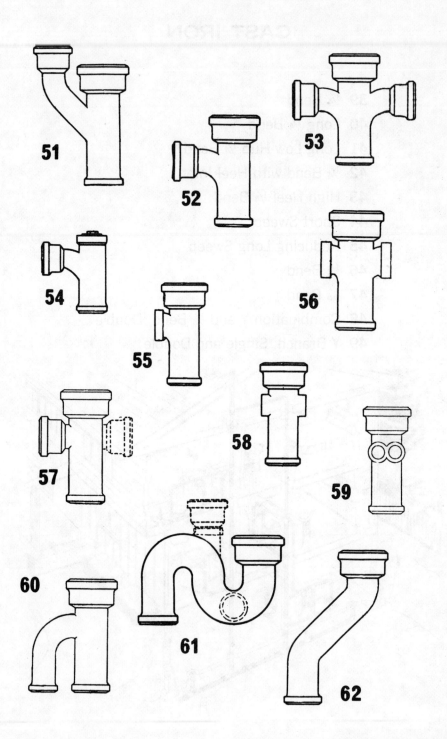

# CAST IRON

51 Y Branch, Upright, Single

52 Sanitary T Branch, Single

53 Sanitary T Branch, Double

54 Sanitary T Branch, Cleanout Plug on Main

55 Sanitary T Branch, Tapped Single

56 Sanitary T Branch, Tapped Double

57 T Branch, Single and Double

58 Tapped T Branch, Double

59 Horizontal Twin Tapped T

60 Vent Branch, Single

61 S Trap, with or without Vent and Cleanout

62 ⅛ Bend Offset.

**DIMENSIONS OF CAST IRON SOIL PIPE IN INCHES**

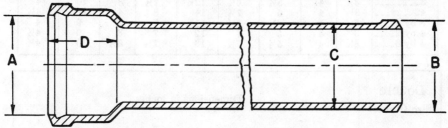

| STANDARD | | | | |
|---|---|---|---|---|
| SIZE | A | B | C | D |
| 2 | 2¹⁵⁄₁₆ | 2⁵⁄₈ | 2¼ | 2½ |
| 3 | 3¹⁵⁄₁₆ | 3⁵⁄₈ | 3¼ | 2¾ |
| 4 | 4¹⁵⁄₁₆ | 4⁵⁄₈ | 4¼ | 3 |

| EXTRA HEAVY | | | | |
|---|---|---|---|---|
| SIZE | A | B | C | D |
| 2 | 3¹⁄₁₆ | 2¾ | 2³⁄₈ | 2½ |
| 3 | 4³⁄₁₆ | 3⁷⁄₈ | 3½ | 2¾ |
| 4 | 5³⁄₁₆ | 4⁷⁄₈ | 4½ | 3 |

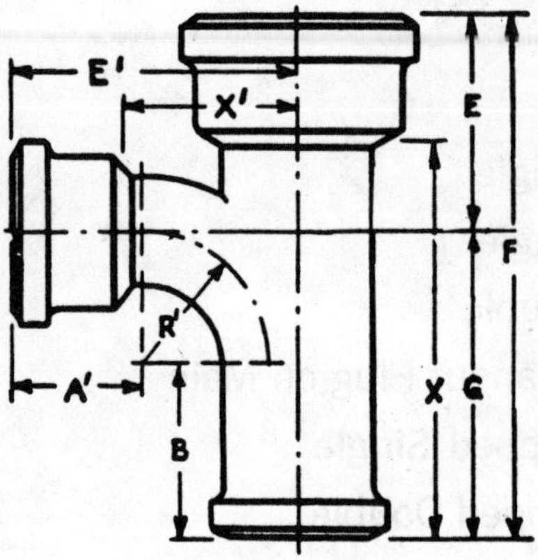


Sanitary T branches, single

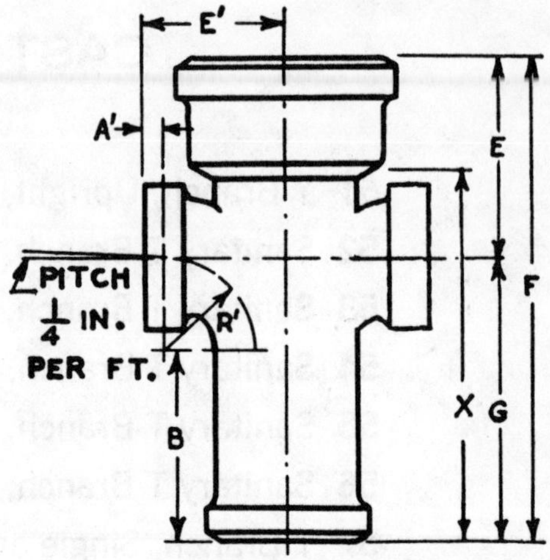


Sanitary T branches, tapped double

| Single Size (inches) | Dimensions in inches | | | | | | | | |
|---|---|---|---|---|---|---|---|---|---|
| | A′ | B | E | E′ | F | G | R′ | X | X′ |
| 2 | 2¾ | 3¾ | 4¼ | 5¼ | 10½ | 6¼ | 2½ | 8 | 2¾ |
| 3 | 3¼ | 4 | 5¼ | 6¾ | 12¾ | 7½ | 3½ | 10 | 4 |
| 4 | 3½ | 4 | 6 | 7½ | 14 | 8 | 4 | 11 | 4½ |
| 3 by 2 | 3 | 4 | 4¾ | 6½ | 11¾ | 7 | 3 | 9 | 4 |
| 4 by 2 | 3 | 4 | 5 | 7 | 12 | 7 | 3 | 9 | 4½ |
| 4 by 3 | 3¼ | 4 | 5½ | 7¼ | 13 | 7½ | 3½ | 10 | 4½ |

| Double Size (inches) | Dimensions in inches | | | | | | | |
|---|---|---|---|---|---|---|---|---|
| | A′ | B | E | E′ | F | G | R′ | X |
| 2 by 2 | 13/16 | 4 | 4¼ | 3 1/16 | 10½ | 6¼ | 2¼ | 8 |
| 3 by 2 | 13/16 | 4¾ | 4¾ | 3 9/16 | 11¾ | 7 | 2¼ | 9 |
| 4 by 2 | 13/16 | 4¾ | 5 | 4 1/16 | 12 | 7 | 2¼ | 9 |

| Size (inches) | B | E′ | R′ |
|---|---|---|---|
| 2 | 4½ | 2 13/16 | 1¾ |
| 3 | 5¼ | 3 5/16 | 1¾ |
| 4 | 5¼ | 3 13/16 | 1¾ |

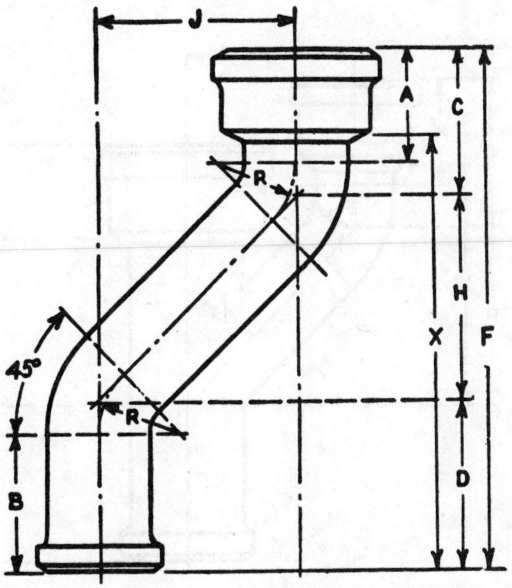


1/8 Bend offset

| Size (inches) | Dimensions in inches | | | | | | | | |
|---|---|---|---|---|---|---|---|---|---|
| | A | B | C | D | F | H | J | R | X |
| 2 by 2 | 2¾ | 3½ | 3½ | 4¼ | 9¾ | 2 | 2 | 2 | 7¼ |
| 2 by 4 | 2¾ | 3½ | 3½ | 4¼ | 11¾ | 4 | 4 | 2 | 9¼ |
| 2 by 6 | 2¾ | 3½ | 3½ | 4¼ | 13¾ | 6 | 6 | 2 | 11¼ |
| 2 by 8 | 2¾ | 3½ | 3½ | 4¼ | 15¾ | 8 | 8 | 2 | 13¼ |
| 2 by 10 | 2¾ | 3½ | 3½ | 4¼ | 17¾ | 10 | 10 | 2 | 15¼ |
| 2 by 12 | 2¾ | 3½ | 3½ | 4¼ | 19¾ | 12 | 12 | 2 | 17¼ |
| 2 by 14 | 2¾ | 3½ | 3½ | 4¼ | 21¾ | 14 | 14 | 2 | 19¼ |
| 2 by 16 | 2¾ | 3½ | 3½ | 4¼ | 23¾ | 16 | 16 | 2 | 21¼ |
| 2 by 18 | 2¾ | 3½ | 3½ | 4¼ | 25¾ | 18 | 18 | 2 | 23¼ |
| 3 by 2 | 3¼ | 4 | 4¼ | 5 | 11¼ | 2 | 2 | 2½ | 8½ |
| 3 by 4 | 3¼ | 4 | 4¼ | 5 | 13¼ | 4 | 4 | 2½ | 10½ |
| 3 by 6 | 3¼ | 4 | 4¼ | 5 | 15¼ | 6 | 6 | 2½ | 12½ |
| 3 by 8 | 3¼ | 4 | 4¼ | 5 | 17¼ | 8 | 8 | 2½ | 14½ |
| 3 by 10 | 3¼ | 4 | 4¼ | 5 | 19¼ | 10 | 10 | 2½ | 16½ |
| 3 by 12 | 3¼ | 4 | 4¼ | 5 | 21¼ | 12 | 12 | 2½ | 18½ |
| 3 by 14 | 3¼ | 4 | 4¼ | 5 | 23¼ | 14 | 14 | 2½ | 20½ |
| 3 by 16 | 3¼ | 4 | 4¼ | 5 | 25¼ | 16 | 16 | 2½ | 22½ |
| 3 by 18 | 3¼ | 4 | 4¼ | 5 | 27¼ | 18 | 18 | 2½ | 24½ |
| 4 by 2 | 3½ | 4 | 4¾ | 5¼ | 12 | 2 | 2 | 3 | 9 |
| 4 by 4 | 3½ | 4 | 4¾ | 5¼ | 14 | 4 | 4 | 3 | 11 |
| 4 by 6 | 3½ | 4 | 4¾ | 5¼ | 16 | 6 | 6 | 3 | 13 |
| 4 by 8 | 3½ | 4 | 4¾ | 5¼ | 18 | 8 | 8 | 3 | 15 |
| 4 by 10 | 3½ | 4 | 4¾ | 5¼ | 20 | 10 | 10 | 3 | 17 |
| 4 by 12 | 3½ | 4 | 4¾ | 5¼ | 22 | 12 | 12 | 3 | 19 |
| 4 by 14 | 3½ | 4 | 4¾ | 5¼ | 24 | 14 | 14 | 3 | 21 |
| 4 by 16 | 3½ | 4 | 4¾ | 5¼ | 26 | 16 | 16 | 3 | 23 |
| 4 by 18 | 3½ | 4 | 4¾ | 5¼ | 28 | 18 | 18 | 3 | 25 |

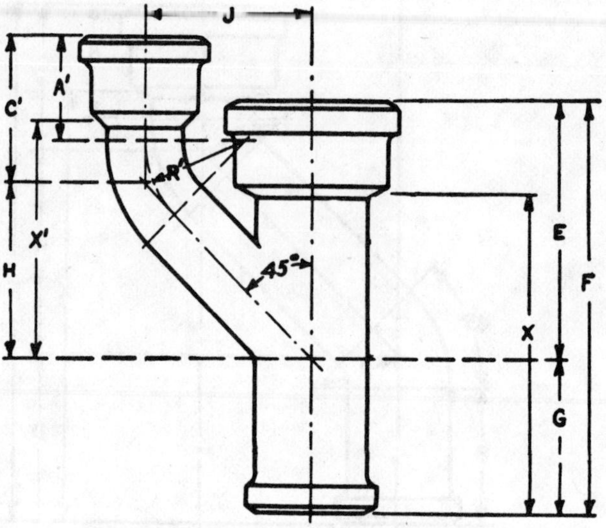


Y branches, upright, single

| Size (inches) | Dimensions in inches | | | | | | | | | |
|---|---|---|---|---|---|---|---|---|---|---|
| | A′ | C′ | E | F | G | H | J | R′ | X | X′ |
| 2 | 2¾ | 4 | 6½ | 10½ | 4 | 4½ | 4½ | 3 | 8 | 6 |
| 3 | 3¼ | 4 11/16 | 8¼ | 13¼ | 5 | 5½ | 5½ | 3½ | 10½ | 7 7/16 |
| 4 | 3½ | 5 3/16 | 9¾ | 15 | 5¼ | 6½ | 6½ | 4 | 12 | 8 11/16 |
| 3 by 2 | 3 | 4¼ | 7 9/16 | 11¾ | 4 3/16 | 5 | 5 | 3 | 9 | 6¾ |
| 4 by 2 | 3 | 4¼ | 8 5/16 | 12 | 3 11/16 | 5½ | 5½ | 3 | 9 | 7¼ |
| 4 by 3 | 3¼ | 4 11/16 | 9 | 13½ | 4½ | 6 | 6 | 3½ | 10½ | 7 15/16 |

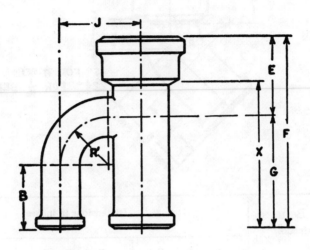

## Vent branches, single

| Size (inches) | Dimensions in inches | | | | | | |
|---|---|---|---|---|---|---|---|
| | B | E | F | G | J | R′ | X |
| 2_____ | 3¼ | 4¼ | 10½ | 6¼ | 4½ | 3 | 8 |
| 3_____ | 4 | 5¼ | 12¾ | 7½ | 5½ | 3½ | 10 |
| 4_____ | 4 | 6 | 14 | 8 | 6½ | 4 | 11 |
| 3 by 2_____ | 4 | 4¾ | 11¾ | 7 | 5 | 3 | 9 |
| 4 by 2_____ | 4 | 5 | 12 | 7 | 5½ | 3 | 9 |
| 4 by 3_____ | 4 | 5½ | 13 | 7½ | 6 | 3½ | 10 |

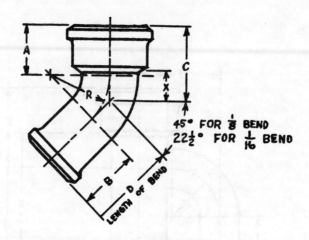

45° FOR 1/8 BEND
22½° FOR 1/16 BEND

| 1/8 Bend<br>Size (inches) | Dimensions in inches | | | | | |
|---|---|---|---|---|---|---|
| | A | B | C | D | R | X |
| 2 | 2¾ | 3 | 4 | 4¼ | 3 | 1½ |
| 3 | 3¼ | 3½ | 4¹¹⁄₁₆ | 4¹⁵⁄₁₆ | 3½ | 1¹⁵⁄₁₆ |
| 4 | 3½ | 4 | 5³⁄₁₆ | 5¹¹⁄₁₆ | 4 | 2³⁄₁₆ |

| Long 1/8 Bends<br>Size (inches) | Dimensions in inches | | | | | |
|---|---|---|---|---|---|---|
| | A | B | C | D | R | X |
| 2 by 12 | 2¾ | 10¾ | 4 | 12 | 3 | 1½ |
| 2 by 18 | 2¾ | 16¾ | 4 | 18 | 3 | 1½ |
| 2 by 24 | 2¾ | 22¾ | 4 | 24 | 3 | 1½ |
| 3 by 12 | 3¼ | 10⁹⁄₁₆ | 4¹¹⁄₁₆ | 12 | 3½ | 1¹⁵⁄₁₆ |
| 3 by 18 | 3¼ | 16⁹⁄₁₆ | 4¹¹⁄₁₆ | 18 | 3½ | 1¹⁵⁄₁₆ |
| 3 by 24 | 3¼ | 22⁹⁄₁₆ | 4¹¹⁄₁₆ | 24 | 3½ | 1¹⁵⁄₁₆ |
| 4 by 12 | 3½ | 10⁵⁄₁₆ | 5³⁄₁₆ | 12 | 4 | 2³⁄₁₆ |
| 4 by 18 | 3½ | 16⁵⁄₁₆ | 5³⁄₁₆ | 18 | 4 | 2³⁄₁₆ |
| 4 by 24 | 3½ | 22⁵⁄₁₆ | 5³⁄₁₆ | 24 | 4 | 2³⁄₁₆ |

| 1/16 Bend<br>Size (inches) | Dimensions in inches | | | | | |
|---|---|---|---|---|---|---|
| | A | B | C | D | R | X |
| 2 | 2¾ | 3 | 3⅜ | 3⅝ | 3 | ⅞ |
| 3 | 3¼ | 3½ | 3¹⁵⁄₁₆ | 4³⁄₁₆ | 3½ | 1³⁄₁₆ |
| 4 | 3½ | 4 | 4⁵⁄₁₆ | 4¹³⁄₁₆ | 4 | 1⁷⁄₁₆ |

## Y branches, single and double

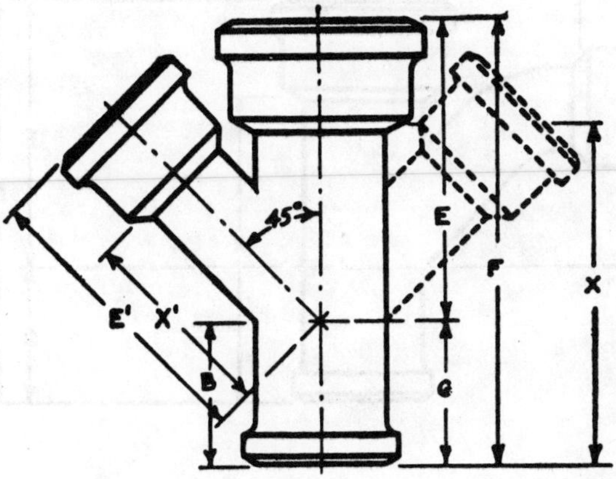


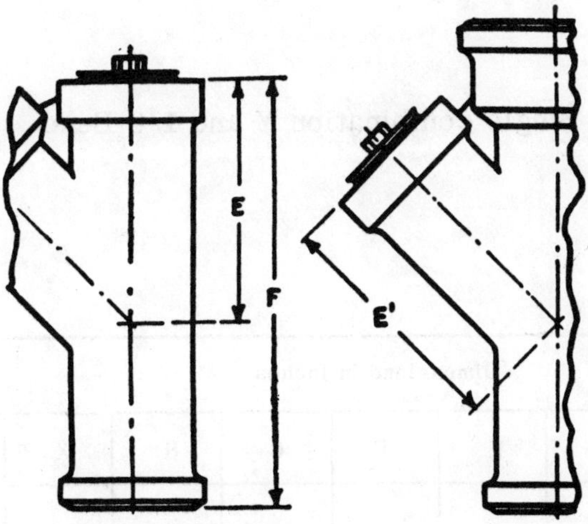


| Size (inches) | Dimensions in inches | | | | | | |
|---|---|---|---|---|---|---|---|
| | B (min.) | E | E′ | F | G | X | X′ |
| 2 | 3½ | 6½ | 6½ | 10½ | 4 | 8 | 4 |
| 3 | 4 | 8¼ | 8¼ | 13¼ | 5 | 10½ | 5½ |
| 4 | 4 | 9¾ | 9¾ | 15 | 5¼ | 12 | 6¾ |
| 3 by 2 | 4 | 7 9/16 | 7½ | 11¾ | 4 3/16 | 9 | 5 |
| 4 by 2 | 4 | 8⅜ | 8¼ | 12 | 3⅝ | 9 | 5¾ |
| 4 by 3 | 4 | 9 1/16 | 9 | 13½ | 4 7/16 | 10½ | 6¼ |

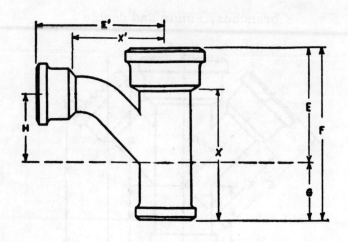

## Single combination Y and 1/8 Bend

| Size (inches) | Dimensions in Inches | | | | | | |
|---|---|---|---|---|---|---|---|
| | E | E′ | F | G | H | X | X′ |
| 2 | 6½ | 7⅜ | 10½ | 4 | 3⅜ | 8 | 4⅞ |
| 3 | 8¼ | 9¾ | 13¼ | 5 | 5¹⁄₁₆ | 10½ | 7 |
| 4 | 9¾ | 12 | 15 | 5¼ | 6¹³⁄₁₆ | 12 | 9 |
| 3 x 2 | 7⁹⁄₁₆ | 8¼ | 11¾ | 4³⁄₁₆ | 4 | 9 | 5¾ |
| 4 x 2 | 8⁵⁄₁₆ | 8¾ | 12 | 3¹¹⁄₁₆ | 4½ | 9 | 6¼ |
| 4 x 3 | 9 | 10¼ | 13½ | 4½ | 5⁹⁄₁₆ | 10½ | 7½ |

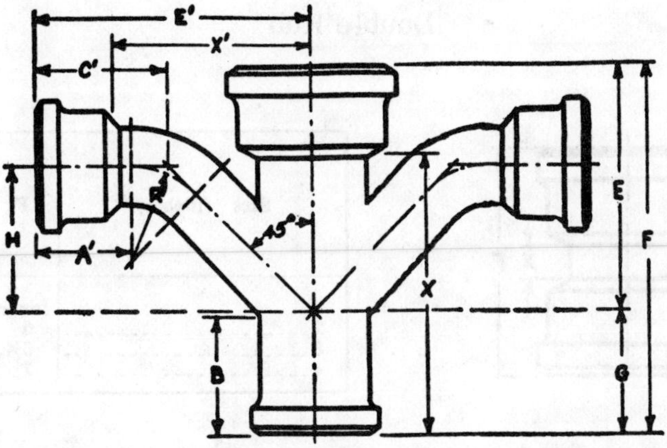


Combination Y and 1/8 bend, double

| Size (inches) | Dimensions in inches | | | | | | | | | | |
|---|---|---|---|---|---|---|---|---|---|---|---|
| | A′ | B min. | C′ | E | E′ | F | G | H | R′ | X | X′ |
| 2 | 2¾ | 3½ | 4 | 6½ | 7⅝ | 10½ | 4 | 3⅝ | 3 | 8 | 4⅞ |
| 3 | 3¼ | 4 | 4 11/16 | 8¼ | 9¾ | 13¼ | 5 | 5 1/16 | 3½ | 10½ | 7 |
| 4 | 3½ | 4 | 5 3/16 | 9¾ | 12 | 15 | 5¼ | 6 13/16 | 4 | 12 | 9 |
| 3 by 2 | 3 | 4 | 4¼ | 7 9/16 | 8¼ | 11¾ | 4 3/16 | 4 | 3 | 9 | 5¾ |
| 4 by 2 | 3 | 4 | 4¼ | 8 5/16 | 8¾ | 12 | 3 11/16 | 4½ | 3 | 9 | 6¼ |
| 4 by 3 | 3¼ | 4 | 4 11/16 | 9 | 10¼ | 13½ | 4½ | 5 9/16 | 3½ | 10½ | 7½ |

Combination Y and 1/8 bend cleanout with screw plug on main

| Size (inches) | Dimensions in inches | | Min. I.P.S. tapping |
|---|---|---|---|
| | E | F | |
| 2 | 5¼ | 9¼ | 1½ |
| 3 | 6⅝ | 11⅝ | 2½ |
| 4 | 7⅞ | 13⅛ | 3½ |

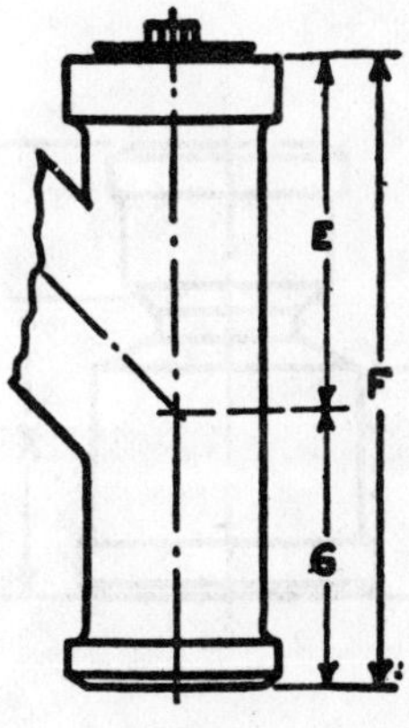

## Double Hub

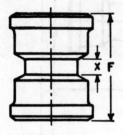

| Size   (inches) | F | X |
|-----------------|---|---|
|                 | Inches | Inch |
| 2-------------------------------------- | 6 | 1 |
| 3-------------------------------------- | 6½ | 1 |
| 4-------------------------------------- | 7 | 1 |

## Long Double Hubs

| Size   (inches) | F | X |
|-----------------|---|---|
|                 | Inches | Inches |
| 2 x 30 | 30 | 25 |
| 3 x 30 | 30 | 24-1/2 |
| 4 x 30 | 30 | 24 |

## Reducers

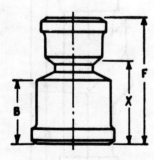

| Size   (inches) | B | F | X |
|-----------------|---|---|---|
|                 | Inches | Inches | Inches |
| 3 by 2------- | 3¾ | 7¼ | 4¾ |
| 4 by 2------- | 4 | 7½ | 5 |
| 4 by 3------- | 4 | 7¾ | 5 |

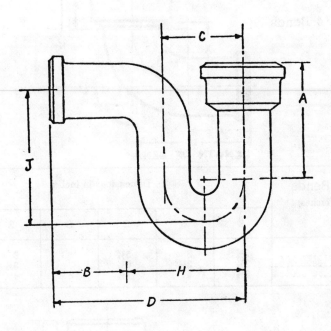

### Deep Seal P Trap

| SIZE (Inches) | Dimension in Inches | | | | | |
|---|---|---|---|---|---|---|
| | A | B | C | D | H | J |
| 2 x 2 | 5 | 3½ | 4 | 9½ | 6 | 6 |
| 3 x 3 | 6 | 4½ | 5 | 12 | 7½ | 7 |
| 4 x 4 | 7 | 4½ | 6 | 14 | 9 | 8 |

## 1/4 Bends

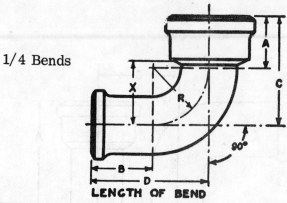

| 1/4 Bends Size (inches) | Dimensions in inches | | | | | |
|---|---|---|---|---|---|---|
| | A | B | C | D | R | X |
| 2 | 2¾ | 3 | 5¾ | 6 | 3 | 3¼ |
| 3 | 3¼ | 3½ | 6¾ | 7 | 3½ | 4 |
| 4 | 3½ | 4 | 7½ | 8 | 4 | 4½ |

## Long 1/4 Bends

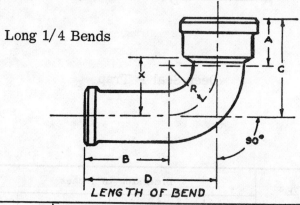

| Long 1/4 Bends Size (inches) | Dimensions in inches | | | | | |
|---|---|---|---|---|---|---|
| | A | B | C | D | R | X |
| 2 by 12 | 2¾ | 9 | 5¾ | 12 | 3 | 3¼ |
| 2 by 18 | 2¾ | 15 | 5¾ | 18 | 3 | 3¼ |
| 2 by 24 | 2¾ | 21 | 5¾ | 24 | 3 | 3¼ |
| 3 by 12 | 3¼ | 8½ | 6¾ | 12 | 3½ | 4 |
| 3 by 18 | 3¼ | 14½ | 6¾ | 18 | 3½ | 4 |
| 3 by 24 | 3¼ | 20½ | 6¾ | 24 | 3½ | 4 |
| 4 by 12 | 3½ | 8 | 7½ | 12 | 4 | 4½ |
| 4 by 18 | 3½ | 14 | 7½ | 18 | 4 | 4½ |
| 4 by 24 | 3½ | 20 | 7½ | 24 | 4 | 4½ |

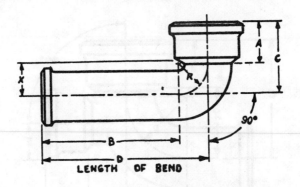

## Long low-hub 1/4 Bends

| Size (inches) | Dimensions in inches | | | | | |
|---|---|---|---|---|---|---|
| | A | B | C | D | R | X |
| 4 by 12 | 3 | 9¼ | 5¾ | 12 | 2¾ | 2¾ |
| 4 by 14 | 3 | 11¼ | 5¾ | 14 | 2¾ | 2¾ |
| 4 by 16 | 3 | 13¼ | 5¾ | 16 | 2¾ | 2¾ |
| 4 by 18 | 3 | 15¼ | 5¾ | 18 | 2¾ | 2¾ |

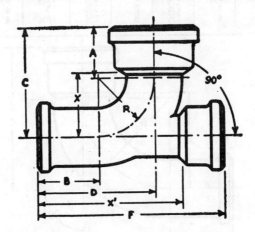

## 1/4 Bend with heel inlet

| Size (inches) | Dimensions in inches | | | | | | | |
|---|---|---|---|---|---|---|---|---|
| | A | B | C | D | F | R | X | X′ |
| 3 by 2 | 3¼ | 3½ | 6¾ | 7 | 11½ | 3½ | 4 | 9 |
| 4 by 2 | 3½ | 4 | 7½ | 8 | 13 | 4 | 4½ | 10½ |
| 4 by 3 | 3½ | 4 | 7½ | 8 | 13¼ | 4 | 4½ | 10½ |

153

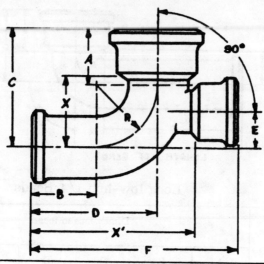

| High heel 1/4 Bends | Dimensions in inches | | | | | | | | |
|---|---|---|---|---|---|---|---|---|---|
| Size (inches) | A | B | C | D | E | F | R | X | X' |
| 3 by 2 | 3¼ | 3½ | 6¾ | 7 | 2¼ | 11½ | 3½ | 4 | 9 |
| 4 by 2 | 3½ | 4 | 7½ | 8 | 2¾ | 13 | 4 | 4½ | 10½ |
| 4 by 3 | 3½ | 4 | 7½ | 8 | 2¼ | 13¼ | 4 | 4½ | 10½ |

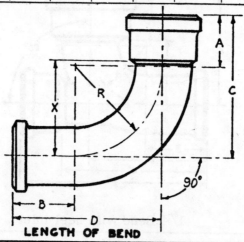

**LENGTH OF BEND**

| Reducing Long Sweep | Dimensions in Inches | | | | | |
|---|---|---|---|---|---|---|
| Size (inches) | A | B | C | D | R | X |
| 3 x 2 | 3 | 3½ | 11½ | 9 | 8½ | 6 |
| 4 x 3 | 3¼ | 4 | 12¼ | 10 | 9 | 6½ |

154

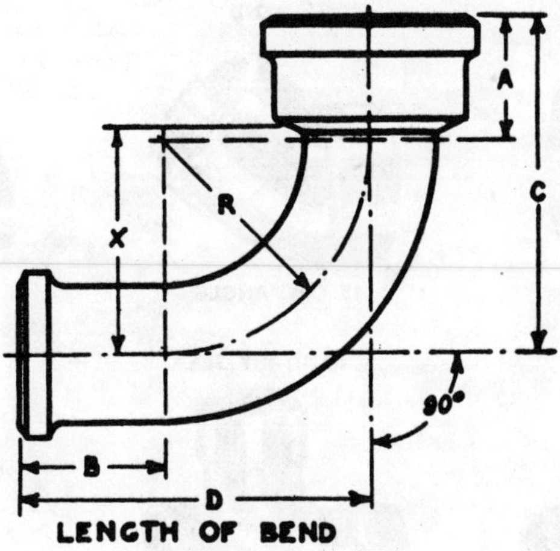
A
C
R
X
90°
B
D
LENGTH OF BEND

Short sweep

| Size (inches) | Dimensions in inches | | | | | |
|---|---|---|---|---|---|---|
| | A | B | C | D | R | X |
| 2 | 2¾ | 3 | 7¾ | 8 | 5 | 5¼ |
| 3 | 3¼ | 3½ | 8¾ | 9 | 5½ | 6 |
| 4 | 3½ | 4 | 9½ | 10 | 6 | 6½ |

Long sweep

| Size (inches) | Dimensions in inches | | | | | |
|---|---|---|---|---|---|---|
| | A | B | C | D | R | X |
| 2 | 2¾ | 3 | 10¾ | 11 | 8 | 8¼ |
| 3 | 3¼ | 3½ | 11¾ | 12 | 8½ | 9 |
| 4 | 3½ | 4 | 12½ | 13 | 9 | 9½ |

# PLASTIC FITTINGS AVAILABLE
## PIPE DIAMETER 2 – 3 – 4 – 6 in.

COUPLING

⅛ BEND

¼ BEND

STRAIGHT

45 Deg. ANGLE

90 Deg. ANGLE

WYE

SANITARY TEE

CAP

45 Deg. ANGLE

90 Deg. ANGLE

90 Deg. SWEEP

45 Deg. SWEEP

MALE ADAPTER to N.P.T.

SPIGOT END OF CLAY PIPE

SOIL PIPE

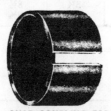

PLASTIC PIPE

PLASTIC PIPE

HUB ADAPTER TO CLAY OR SOIL PIPE

SNAP COUPLING FOR PERFORATED PIPE

CLAY SPIGOT ADAPTER

FIBER PIPE

PLASTIC PIPE

For 2" x 3" leader; also available for 3" x 4" leader.

(each coupling reduces one size)
PIPE DIAMETER 3"-4"-6"

DOWNSPOUT ADAPTER

REDUCING COUPLING

ADAPTER FOR FIBER PIPE

CLEAN-OUT BUSHING
PIPE DIAMETER 3"-4"

THREADED PLUG

PLASTIC PIPE
CAST IRON PIPE
LEAD SPIGOT
ADAPTER TO CAST
IRON SOIL PIPE
PIPE DIAMETER 4"

CROSS

When assembling threaded plastic pipe always use a strap wrench, Illus. 87, rather than a pipe wrench. Never use pliers. Don't overtighten a fitting. Threaded plastic pipe is always joined hand tight plus one to one and a half turns. To make certain you know how many turns are required, dry fit pipe and fitting. Count the number of turns needed to hand tighten. Remove fitting from pipe. Apply tape or dope to male thread only.

Screw fitting onto pipe using the same number of turns as previously required. Now turn the fitting, using a strap wrench, one to one and a half turns beyond the hand tightened point.

CAUTION. Keep solvent cans covered when not in use. Don't use welding solvent compounds after they begin to gel or thicken. Do not add thinners. Throw it away and get a new can of the welding solvent pipe manufacturer recommends. Never attempt to assemble pipe in freezing or below freezing temperature or when pipe or fitting is wet.

## PLASTIC HIGH TEMPERATURE PIPE

You can make professional plumbing repairs to hot and cold water lines with high temperature plastic pipe if you follow certain basic rules.

1. Always cut pipe clean, remove burrs, clean pipe and fitting with a cloth dampened with cleaner manufacturer recommends.
2. Brush on solvent, join, twist and allow to set as described previously.
3. Support pipe every 32" with clamps recommended by plastic pipe manufacturer. These permit pipe to expand

157

with heat, contract with cold. Never clamp plastic, copper
or any material that expands and contracts too securely.
You must allow it to move freely.

## TRANSITION ADAPTER

(Note: Do not enclose transition fittings in walls or other inaccessible places as a matter of good
plumbing practice.)

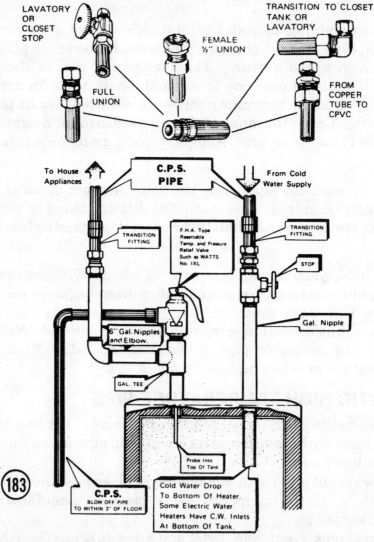

One leading manufacturer of high temperature water pipe offers color
coded pipe. The hot water side can be orange, the cold water green. Illus.
183 shows how galvanized nipples, elbows and tee are installed in a hot
water heater then connected to high temperature plastic.

# GLOSSARY OF WORDS USED IN PLUMBING

**FSPS**   Female standard pipe size.

**MPT**   Male pipe thread.

**MSPS**   Male standard pipe size.

**ADAPTER**   A fitting used to connect two different size pipe or fitting. For example: Soil Pipe Adapter joins cast iron soil pipe hub to 3″, 2″ or 1½″ copper tube, Illus. 33, 67, 68. Available in many different sizes in both male and female.
Male adapter, Illus. 95, p. 69, is designated copper to MSPS (Male Standard Pipe Size). Joins copper tube to female pipe thread. Also note Illus. 93, p. 67.

**BACKING BOARD**   Usually a 1x4, 1x6 or 1x8 nailed flush with leading edge of studs to provide support for a fixture, Illus. 2, 49, 51, 52.

**BATHTUB INSTALLATION**   overflow pipe and drain, Illus. 89, 90.

**BIDET**   (pronounced be-day) Illus. 22. A fixture that cleanses the essentials. For lovers.

**BRANCH**   Any vent or drainage pipe other than soil or vent stack, Illus. 31.

**BRIDGING**   A support or nailor nailed between joists or studs. Solid bridging, Illus. 46.

**CALKING**   Also spelled caulking. Material like oakum and lead, Illus. 24.

**CALKING TOOLS**   iron, plumbers furnace, lead pot, ladle, Illus. 26.

**CAST IRON**   Hub and Spigot, Illus. 24; no-hub, Illus. 27; compression type, Illus. 28.

**CAST IRON CALKING RUNNER**   Asbestos rope clamp, Illus. 76. Permits pouring lead in horizontal hub and spigot joint.

**CAST IRON PLUMBING TREE**   Illus. 31.

**CAST IRON PIPE CUTTER**   Illus. 86.

**CAT**   Short piece of lumber, usually 2x4, nailed between studs to back up edge of gypsum board or fixture, Illus. 2.

**CHASE**   Recess cut in framing to permit installing pipe, Illus. 4

**CLEANOUT PLUG**   cast iron, Illus. 33.

**CLOSET BEND**   Illus. 4, 15, 31, 55. For other installations, note Illus. 57, 72, 73.

**CLOSET FLANGE**   Illus. 4, 15, 31; also called floor flange.

**CLOSET SCREW**   Long screw with detachable head formerly in wide use for fastening water closet to floor.

**COMPRESSION GASKET**   for cast iron hub, Illus. 28.

**COMPRESSION NUT ADAPTER**   Illus. 101.

**CORNER TOILET**   Illus. 17, p. 24.

**COUPLING**   Illus. 99, p. 70. A coupling joins two pieces of pipe of the same or different sizes. Some couplings have stops to allow pipe to only go in so far; others have no stop. Also available Copper to Slip-Joint, Illus. 101, p. 72

**DIVERTER VALVE**   bathtub and shower control. Connects to hot and cold water line, Illus. 49, 50, 51, 93, 94, 134.

**DRAINAGE**   Any pipe that carries waste water in the drainage system.

159

**DROP EAR ELBOW 90°** Illus. 96, p. 69. ½" x ¾". Permits connecting copper shower supply line to threaded nipple required for shower head.

**DRUM TRAP** recommended for bathtub installation, Illus. 31, 92.

**DWV FITTINGS** these drainage, waste and vent fittings incorporate the recommended drainage pitch of ¼" to the foot.

**ELL — L — ELBOW** a Quarter Bend 90°, Illus. 4.

**ESCUTCHEON** A plate used to enclose pipe or fitting at wall or floor opening.

**FEMALE** end of fitting that receives male.

**FERRULE** a threaded sleeve soldered to hub of pipe, Illus. 33.

**FITTINGS** Any coupling, tee, elbow, union, etc., other than pipe. Plumbing catalogs refer to fittings as "ftg."

**FIXTURE PLACEMENT CHART** Illus. 48, p. 44. Scale drawings and layout grid, p. 121, 159.

**FIXTURE UNIT** A method of estimating amount of water a fixture discharges. A unit is equivalent to 7½ gallons of water or one cubic foot of water per minute. While a bathroom containing toilet, lavatory, bathtub or shower stall is rated by national codes as 6 units, the same codes rate a bathtub with 1½" trap, with or without shower, 2 units; with 2" trap — 3 units; a bidet —3 units; lavatory —1 unit; shower stall —2 units; an extra toilet with 3" drain — 4 units.

**FPT** Indicates female pipe thread.

**FRAMING** walls for bathroom, Illus. 45, 47; end of bathtub, Illus. 21.

**FRESH AIR INLET** Pipe above roof, Illus. 160, 165, p. 116, 117. Codes frequently require this be size larger than internal vent line.

**INCREASER** A coupling with one end larger than the other, Illus. 30, p. 136. Used to increase diameter of pipe above roof.

**INSPECTION PANEL** provides access to bathtub trap, Illus. 53.

**KAYFER** Also called Kafir. A screw type hub fitting on cast iron that simplifies making new connection in 4" soil line, p. 54, 60, 61.

**LAVATORY P TRAP** Illus. 31, p. 31.

**LEAD BEND** formerly used exclusively as a closet connection to soil line. We don't recommend same as it's easier to install closet bends illustrated.

**MALE** End of fitting that inserts in female.

**NO-HUB CAST IRON** Illus. 27.

**OFFSET** Note ⅛ Bend Offset, Illus. 31; also any combination of pipe and fitting, or combination of fittings used to angle over.

**PARTITION** end of tub, Illus. 21; privacy partition, Illus. 19.

**PIPE CUTTER** cast iron, Illus. 34; copper, Illus. 35, p. 33.

**PIPE MARKER** insures sawing pipe square, Illus. 87.

**PIPE SIZING CHART** Illus. 23, p. 27. Simplifies sizing existing pipes.

**PIPE STRAP** Illus. 4.

**PLASTIC PIPE** p. 156.

**PLUMBING TOOLS** Illus. 26, 87.

**PRE-ENGINEERED PLUMBING WALL** a completely assembled plumbing wall, Illus. 8. p. 15.

**PRE-FABRICATED BATHROOM** Illus. 6, p. 13.

**REDUCER** Copper to copper, Illus. 8, p. 15. Joins ¾" to ½". Also available in other sizes.

**ROOF VENT INCREASER** Illus. 28, p. 136. Fitting simplifies increasing vent from 3" to 4". Available 3" x 4" in 18", 24", 30" lengths.

160

**ROUGH-IN** This describes installation of drainage waste and supply lines. Roughing-in concerns all work required prior to connecting fixtures.

**SANITARY TEE 90° WITH SLIP JOINT** Illus. 5, p. 132. Joins copper waste and vent line to chrome or brass lavatory or sink drain pipe. Nut tightens lead ring to make tight joint.

**SLIP JOINT** Illus. 101, p. 72.

**SOIL STACK** Codes allow 3″ or 4″ cast iron, copper, plastic, Illus. 4.

**SOIL LINE LAYOUT GUIDE** use folding rule or garden hose, Illus. 54.

**SOIL PIPE** carries discharge from one or more toilets and/or discharge from other fixtures to main sewer line.

**SOLDER CUP END** Illus. 14, p. 135.

**SPIGOT** end of pipe that fits into hub, Illus. 24, p. 28.

**STACK VENT OR VENT STACK** that part of the soil stack above the highest drain connected to stack, see Illus. 31.

**STOP, VALVE** Available in angle and straight stops, Illus. 116, 117, p. 81. Permits shutting off supply to fixture when repairs are required.

**TOILET** roughing-in, Illus. 44.

**TRAP** A fitting designed to provide a liquid seal to prevent back passage of air, note P-Trap, Drum Trap, House Trap, Illus. 31, p. 31.

**TUBE BENDER** tool simplifies bending soft copper tubing, Illus. 87.

**TUBE STRAP** Illus. 50, p. 45; Illus. 60, p. 51.

**VENT STACK** this is a vertical pipe that provides circulation of air to branch vents, re-vents or individual vents. Illus. 31.

**WALL HUNG TOILET** Illus. 9.

**WASTE** this refers to water from any fixture except toilet.

**WASTE PIPE** one that conveys only liquids, no fecal matter.

**WET VENT** a wet vent is both a vent and drainage line from any fixture except a toilet, Illus. 37, p. 35.

**Y-BRANCH** Illus. 31, p. 31.